To Keep the Republic

To Keep the Republic

Thinking, Talking, and Acting

Like a Democratic Citizen

ELIZABETH C. MATTO

RUTGERS UNIVERSITY PRESS

NEW BRUNSWICK, CAMDEN, AND NEWARK, NEW JERSEY

LONDON AND OXFORD

Rutgers University Press is a department of Rutgers, The State University of New Jersey, one of the leading public research universities in the nation. By publishing worldwide, it furthers the University's mission of dedication to excellence in teaching, scholarship, research, and clinical care.

Library of Congress Cataloging-in-Publication Data

Names: Matto, Elizabeth C., author.
Title: To keep the republic : thinking, talking, and acting like a democratic citizen / Elizabeth C. Matto.
Description: New Brunswick : Rutgers University Press, 2024. | Includes bibliographical references and index.
Identifiers: LCCN 2023035831 | ISBN 9781978829701 (paperback) | ISBN 9781978829718 (hardback) | ISBN 9781978829725 (epub) | ISBN 9781978829732 (pdf)
Subjects: LCSH: Political participation—United States. | Deliberative democracy—United States. | United States—Politics and government. | BISAC: POLITICAL SCIENCE / Political Process / Political Advocacy | POLITICAL SCIENCE / American Government / General
Classification: LCC JK1764 .M383 2024 | DDC 323.6/50973—dc23/eng/20231120
LC record available at https://lccn.loc.gov/2023035831

A British Cataloging-in-Publication record for this book is available from the British Library.

rutgersuniversitypress.org

To teachers of democracy, in word and deed.

Contents

Foreword

Not so long ago—perhaps as recently as a decade—a guide to democratic citizenship exploring how we can "keep the republic" might have seemed hyperbolic, if not unnecessary. After all, the United States has been the longest-lasting republic in world history, with the longest-lasting Constitution and a tradition of respecting that Constitution by effecting peaceful transitions of power. Historian Michael Kammen, in his Reagan-era classic *A Machine That Would Go of Itself: The Constitution in American Culture*, described Americans' faith in the unique durability of our republic as almost religious in its unquestioning belief.

As I write this foreword in September 2022, however, that faith, which Kammen warned was too often a faith born of ignorance, has been shaken. To say that American democracy is in crisis is not hyperbole; it is fact. To wonder aloud if we can keep it is not an idle exercise; it is an immediate concern. To provide a clear nonpartisan blueprint for engagement in a democratic republic is not only timely; it is urgent. Hence the value to our moment and to our future of Professor Elizabeth Matto's book *To Keep the Republic*.

The question that haunts our republic as I write this foreword is whether the events of January 6, 2021, were a culmination or a prelude. The answer to that question will define our future as a republic. Indeed, one of the few things about which Republicans and Democrats agree is that the threat to our republic is the number one issue facing our nation, eclipsing climate change, inflation, and the armed conflict in Ukraine.[1]

The consensus ends there. Our airwaves are filled with experts and partisans on all sides bewailing our polarization, despairing of America's future, and mostly pointing fingers and screaming at the other side for causing this sorry state of affairs. Lots of heat, very little light.

But what I saw displayed on January 6, and was reflected in survey after survey of public attitudes, required not rhetoric but instruction; it was ignorance plain and simple. Ignorance of how our Constitution is supposed to work; of the commitment of thousands of state and local election officials, and hundreds of judges, to administer our elections fairly, and in doing so to uphold our Constitution. In the aftermath of January 6, the Joint Chiefs of Staff felt compelled to issue a letter reminding members of our armed forces that their oath is to preserve, protect, and defend the Constitution. Alarm bells were sounded at every level of mainstream media and American higher education about the vast ignorance of the principles of our government among American citizens.[2]

In retrospect, however, the warning signs had been abundant. Studies conducted over the past several years revealed that when it comes to knowledge of the rudiments of American government and the democratic process, Americans have become illiterate. A 2014 survey by the Annenberg Public Policy Center at the University of Pennsylvania, for instance, revealed that only 36 percent of respondents could name all three branches of government (Congress, the president, and the Supreme Court). A 2012 study by Xavier University exposed that only about 60 percent of native-born Americans were able to pass the citizenship test administered to immigrants, compared with the immigrant pass rate of 97.5 percent. Current citizens scored especially poorly on that part of the exam about the Constitution and American law and government. Eighty-five percent of native-born Americans did not know the meaning of "the rule of law," and 71 percent were unable to identify the Constitution as "the supreme law of the land."

It is little wonder that a January 6 can happen when nearly half of the adult American public cannot pass the citizenship test passed by over 90 percent of immigrants; ignorance of democratic values and norms provides fertile ground for disinformation, conspiracy theories, and the demagogues who promote them. What our country desperately needs, therefore, is someone to teach us, someone to remind us what it takes to be an engaged participant in our republic.

Elizabeth Matto's book provides that essential lesson. Professor Matto, a research professor at the Eagleton Institute of Politics at Rutgers University and for fifteen years director of the Institute's Center for Youth Political Participation, is an expert not just in the political science of republican governance but in its pedagogy and practice. In groundbreaking courses at Rutgers such as "Talking Politics: Disagreeing without Being Disagreeable," and in programs encouraging civic engagement such as RU Voting and RU Ready, she has explored the intersection of theory and practice in politics, and brings that deep reservoir of theory and practice to bear in *To Keep the Republic*.

Her book is essential reading for anyone—of any ideological persuasion—who is concerned for the future of our republic. For above all it counsels an appreciation of what it means to be a democratic citizen and a vision of engaged citizenship in our democracy. May it be read far and wide by high school, college and graduate students, and—perhaps more important—by our perplexed adult population. Common ground does indeed exist; if nowhere else, may we find it in Professor Matto's wise and humane vision for keeping our republic.

—Christine Todd Whitman
September 20, 2022

CHRISTINE TODD WHITMAN was the 50th governor of the State of New Jersey. She was elected governor in 1993, becoming the first woman to hold that office in New Jersey.

Preface

When I was approached by Rutgers University Press in 2019 about writing something along the lines of a guide or a primer on the essential elements of democratic citizenship, it seemed a perfect extension of my work both in the classroom and out. Much of my career has been spent at an institute of politics where our mission is to link the study of American politics with its practice, with the aim of improving democracy and promoting political participation and civic engagement.[1] A political scientist by training, my interest always has been in applied scholarship, teaching, and service—all with the hope of making politics and the nation's democratic system better.

In the classroom and as director of the Center for Youth Political Participation,[2] this mission has been pursued by guiding students in an inquiry into how we theorize democracy and how we actually practice it in the United States—identifying the points of resonance and dissonance. Whenever possible, this inquiry has extended outside the classroom and into the community. Not only do I want students to read and discuss the scholarship related to electoral law and its impact on youth political participation, for instance; I want students to experience it by administering voter registration drives for their peers and working to get out the vote.

Over the course of my career, the scholarship associated with teaching civic engagement has advanced and taken on greater prominence in the discipline of political science, and I've been fortunate to be involved in three publications by the American Political Science Association (APSA) dedicated to teaching democracy.[3]

So when Rutgers University Press reached out, I felt well equipped to take on the task of distilling and sharing the essential elements of American democracy (both how we conceive of it and how we practice it). My thought was to reach an audience of varying ages and stages of understanding— whether the audience was advanced high school students supplementing their study of American history with lessons in active citizenship, college students in the early stages of their academic career just becoming familiar with the academic literature on political engagement and seeking ways to apply this learning to real life, civic-minded organizations engaged in the grassroots work of mobilizing citizens who want to ground their work in existing research and theoretical frameworks, citizens who either never received this background throughout their academic career (as civic education has become less and less prevalent in schooling, this is often the case with recent generations), or those who may have studied civics and democratic thought at some point but whose current appreciation is incomplete or even misguided.

I never could have imagined at the time how important the work of teaching democratic citizenship would be for students and the public at large. Indeed, events of the last few years have led many of us to question not only our commitment to American democracy, but even our commitment to our fellow citizens.

In just the past few years, the nation has experienced:

- A twice-impeached presidential administration whose time in office (and even post-presidency) was marked by defiance of democratic norms and constitutional principles;
- A global pandemic that has left over one million dead in the United States, upended the economy, laid bare social and economic inequities, and pitted federal, state, and local authorities against one another as they respond to the health emergency;
- Ignited by the killing of George Floyd by a Minneapolis police officer, a long-overdue collective reckoning with the structural racism embedded in the nation's past and present;
- An unprecedented presidential election that, despite numerous court proceedings affirming its legitimacy, has been vigorously contested through media outlets and such extralegal procedures as "election audits" by private contractors;[4]
- Persistent legislative battles in Congress and in state legislatures across the country over voting practices and the fundamental access to the ballot;[5]

- A pervasive partisan toxicity that seems to cloud everything—the halls of government, the airwaves, social media platforms, science, the college campus, the schoolhouse, the workplace, the neighborhood, and even the family home.

Of course, it's not as if threats to democracy or tension among the citizenry are without precedent or without historical or institutional roots. It's also worth acknowledging the tremendous democratic progress the nation has made throughout its history and the moments of unity and comity it has witnessed—more to come on these points throughout the book. Still, the United States seems to be at an inflection point—one that could lead the nation closer to the ideals we claim to embody or further away.

My hope is to play a role in making democracy better. Indeed, although nonpartisan, *To Keep the Republic* is pro-democratic . . . lower-case "d" . . . and aims to provide a sort of roadmap for what American democracy might be . . . not always guided by our past but at least by our possibility. As Winston Churchill expressed, "Many forms of Government have been tried, and will be tried in this world of sin and woe. No one pretends that democracy is perfect or all-wise. Indeed it has been said that democracy is the worst form of Government except for all those other forms that have been tried from time to time."[6] A democratic form of government still offers the best route for securing and advancing the innate rights of the individual and the good of the populace as a whole. In short, it's worth it "to keep the republic."

To Keep the Republic

CHAPTER 1

To Keep the Republic

When seeking insight into the American experience or pearls of wisdom about American democracy, we often look to Benjamin Franklin. We look to Franklin not only to better understand the nation's roots but also to make sense of the realities of today. The story goes that Franklin, upon emerging from the Constitutional Convention in 1787, was asked whether the resulting governmental system crafted by the Framers was a republic or a monarchy, to which Franklin reportedly replied, "A republic, if you can keep it."

This quote often has been used to shine a light on the fragility of American democracy, but the accuracy of the story is not entirely clear. Historians have pointed out that the quote doesn't appear in writing anywhere—not in Franklin's writings, in transcripts of the Convention, or in newspapers.[1] Others have pointed out that the story surrounding the quote has evolved over the years and may have been the product of a conversation Franklin had with prominent Philadelphia socialite Elizabeth Willing Powel.[2] American folklore or not,

Franklin's sentiment resonates . . . the success of the United States' republican form of government is not guaranteed, and it is the people's responsibility to preserve it.

The United States often has been described as a "democratic experiment." American democracy was a product of the Enlightenment era, a philosophical period that emphasized reason and the individual. As a representative democracy rooted in the people, it offered an alternative to aristocratic governmental structures that linked political power to class and heredity. This was a unique form of self-government though, one built upon and shaped by a written Constitution.

Although it offers a way to organize government, American democracy also can be thought of as an ethos, even a way of life. As Walt Whitman asserted in *Democratic Vistas*, the true democratic spirit must extend beyond the mechanics of voting on Election Day and permeate all facets of culture. "Did you too, O friend, suppose democracy was only for elections, politics, and for a party name? I say democracy is only of use there that it may pass on and come to its flower and fruits in manners, in the highest forms of interaction between men, and their beliefs—in Religion, Literature, colleges and schools—Democracy in all public and private life, and in the Army and Navy."[3]

Like Whitman, I hold in this book that American democracy is expansive in nature and that democratic citizenship (lower-case "d") is multifaceted and pervasive. Indeed, democratic citizenship is about much more than party identification and candidate choices; it's about embodying democracy's

Figure 1. Independence Hall. Courtesy of the National Park Service.

ideals not just on Election Day but every day. On that note, I intend the terms "citizen" and "citizenship" to be considered expansively also. The word origins of "citizen" conceptualize the term as one who inhabits a city or town, or "a civilian" rather than a representative of the state. To be sure, there are certain activities, such as voting, that require a legal "citizenship" status. More often than not, though, the job of "keeping the republic" can and must be taken up by all of us, and it is this spirit that animates the text. To preserve and sustain American democracy, what is required is not necessarily a similarity of opinion but a common understanding of what it means to be part of American democracy and a willingness to put that understanding into practice. What it takes to "keep the republic"—how to think, talk, and act like a democratic citizen—is the focus of this book.

THE STATE OF AMERICAN DEMOCRACY

American democracy is at a crossroads, and the success of the "democratic experiment" is in question. Apparent beacon around the world, the United States' democratic system is now seen as vulnerable, in decline, and being eclipsed by other nations around the world.[4] Growing louder in recent years, alarm bells about the nation's democratic health reached a crescendo with the violent attack on the Capitol on January 6, 2021, in an attempt to overturn the outcome of a fair election. In signing a "statement of concern," scholars of democracy asserted that they viewed "the recent deterioration of U.S. elections and liberal democracy with growing alarm," and declared that "our entire democracy is now at risk."[5] The attack on the Capitol was certainly not the only evidence of the fragility of democracy, though.[6] Troubling signs surround not only how we vote in the United States but also how we talk to each other, and even how we conceive of the nation's core ideals.

- Americans consistently vote at lower rates than counterparts in similarly situated democracies, with turnout rates particularly low in the midterm elections, primaries, and state and local races.[7] Moreover, in numerous ways, the pool of regular voters doesn't reflect the demographics of the populace, with notable gaps in turnout by level of income, race and ethnicity, and level of education.[8]
- In what seems like a distortion of the right to speak freely, peaceably assemble, and petition the government for grievances enshrined in the First Amendment, Americans

are increasingly unable to talk to each other, demonstrate an unwillingness to engage with those who disagree with us politically, and rarely find common ground after a discussion with someone from another party.[9]

• Agreement about the nation's core values and how well the country upholds them even seems to break along partisan lines. The Pew Research Center found that 74 percent of Republicans and those who leaned Republican believed the phrase "everyone has an equal opportunity to succeed" described the country well, compared to 37 percent of Democrats and those who lean Democratic. Similarly, 60 percent of those aligning with the Republican Party thought the phrase "the rights and freedoms of all people are respected" accurately represented the nation today, compared to 38 percent of Democrats.[10]

Although everyday Americans may not be in the halls of government making the decisions that affect such democratic practices as voting or passing legislation that affects our everyday lives, the power to put these decision makers in office lies with the people. Once in office, it is the job of the citizen to hold these officeholders accountable—sometimes by meeting with them or sending an email of encouragement or criticism, and sometimes by protesting in the streets. Such accountability can only take place when the populace is informed and curious—consuming news critically and being willing to engage with a diversity of opinions. Finally, this willingness to look honestly not only at the nation's present but also its history, and to view each other as equal participants in the democratic process, requires a shared appreciation of the nation's ideals. Although American democracy is far from perfect in design and practice, the ultimate burden is on the citizens to "keep the republic," and maintaining it requires a full understanding of citizenship. *To Keep the Republic* is meant to respond to this need.

PLAN OF THE BOOK

Written for those who haven't yet learned them and for those who may have forgotten them, *To Keep the Republic* outlines the essential elements of democratic citizenship and explains their importance in preserving the republic's health and longevity. The aim of this book is to identify and explore the different facets of democratic citizenship that compose the nation's democratic ethos and way of life; synthesize and translate relevant theoretical frameworks and scholarship regarding these facets of citizenship; investigate how and where the nation is meeting its democratic ideals and where we're falling short; and finally, explore how and where "we the people" can not only meet our democratic ideals but exceed them . . . going beyond what we are expected to be as a democracy, but even achieving what we might be.

The book begins with an exploration in chapter 2 of the philosophical roots of American democratic thinking and contemporary theoretical frameworks of democratic citizenship, emphasizing that a shared understanding of the core values composing the spirit of democratic citizenship is necessary for the health and longevity of the republic. Subsequent chapters address the different elements of democratic citizenship critical to maintaining the republic. Chapter 3 looks at the role of political discourse, or talking like a democratic citizen. This chapter explores the links between freedom of expression and self-government, asserting that, just like voting and staying informed, democratic citizenship entails a willingness and a facility with engaging in political discussion. Chapter 4 turns to election behavior and explores the many ways in which residents of all ages and backgrounds can play an active role in determining who is elected to office—not only voting, but making campaign contributions and volunteering on a campaign. Not only do democratic citizens determine who sits in office, they influence their actions. Chapter 5 explores methods and the impact of speaking out on officeholders and the consequences for political actions when only segments of the populace express their political voice. It is often said that democracy is not a spectator sport—it requires doing. It is a nation of "doers," then, that keeps a system of self-government authentic, with citizens who not only volunteer their time and resources to address public problems but who also are willing to extend themselves by serving on boards and commissions and running for office—these forms of engagement also serve as the focal point of chapter 5. Finally, chapter 6 explores a moment in literary history that serves to illuminate the core themes of *To Keep the Republic*—the decision of Langston Hughes, leading poet of the Harlem Renaissance, to speak at the Walt Whitman House and defend Whitman later in his life. The story offers an example, not just in art but also in politics, of how to acknowledge human failings while continuing to strive toward higher aspirations—artistic and even democratic.

In her address to the Democratic National Convention in 1976, Congresswoman Barbara Jordan (the first Black woman to deliver a keynote address at a national party convention) articulated the sort of quest for an aspirational version of democracy that this book considers. She stated, "We are a people in a quandary about the present. We are a people in search of our future. We are a people in search of a national community. We are a people trying not only to solve the problems of the present, . . . but we are attempting on a larger scale to fulfill the promise of America. We are attempting to fulfill our national purpose, to create and sustain a society in which all of us are equal."

Much like this text, Congresswoman Jordan envisioned the citizen as a key player in this endeavor, "A nation is formed by the willingness of each of us to share in the responsibility for upholding the common good. A government is invigorated when each one of us is willing to participate in shaping the future of this nation."[11]

Ultimately, it depends on the people who compose it "to keep the republic."

CHAPTER 2

Thinking Like a Democratic Citizen

In the 1830s, the young French aristocrat Alexis de Tocqueville traveled to the United States and observed the nation's fledgling governmental system in action. At the time, his nation and others were beginning to transform from feudal systems rooted in aristocracy to democratic systems in which power was vested in the people. Transformations from aristocracies to democracies in Europe then had been marked by violence, often resulting in unstable systems. His original intent was to study the new nation's penal system, but instead, Tocqueville found himself studying Americans' approach to civic life and the functioning of this new system of government.

Tocqueville's experiences in the United States led him to assert in his text *Democracy in America* that the nation offered a promising model for democracies that were emerging around the world—not solely because of its governmental structures and processes, but because of its mores, norms, and way of thinking. He wrote, "I confess that in America I have seen more than America itself; I have looked there for an image of the essence of democracy, its inclinations, its personality, its prejudices, its passions."[1] It was this democratic sensibility that provided the new nation its stability, Tocqueville concluded, and it is this democratic sensibility that serves as the focal point of this chapter.

Characterizing American democracy as "experimental" implicitly assumes that its success is not guaranteed. Its fragility is suggested in Franklin's description of the nation's system as "a republic, if you can keep it." It's safe to say, then, that in order for American democracy to thrive and survive, a shared understanding not only of how it works but why it works the way it does is required. In short, democracy's health is inextricably linked to our understanding of democracy, and what's required then is that participants in American democracy *think* like democratic citizens.

This chapter synthesizes what are widely regarded as the essential elements of American democratic thought, identifying their roots and exploring how they are appreciated today. This exercise reveals tensions or inherent contradictions within the body of American democratic thought. The foundational value of liberty is a complex one, a democratic value that doesn't necessarily hold primacy among all other values, but a value that can only flourish if the democratic value of equality also is secured. Similarly, diversity of opinion and even the competition of interests is the lifeblood of the United States, but compromise and unity also are expected. Political participation and the "power of the people" are central notions but exist alongside the rule of law and a set of principles codified in a written Constitution.

These inherent contradictions in our thinking reflect the historical and institutional disjunctures that pervade the American democratic experience. Foremost, we must confront the reality that the same individuals who authored the seminal phrase "We hold these Truths to be self-evident, that all men are created equal" also themselves enslaved human beings. Indeed, slavery is interwoven through America's history, and the nation continues to struggle with making equality a reality. Inconsistencies between ideals and reality also are evident in the way the nation's political system is structured. The "winner take all" electoral system used to determine representation in Congress, for example, has been a contributing factor in the entrenched partisanship that dominates American politics today, making compromise and unity seemingly impossible.

The ostensible goal of self-government is civic participation and an active citizenry, and such action is critical to the success of a representative democracy. What also is critical, though, is a shared commitment to facilitate such participation and enable *all* citizens access to political power. Although vocalizing our beliefs and seeking to advance our interests are part of our civic toolkit, American democracy also expects that we'll strive toward cohesion and aim for the good of the populace as a whole. Although sovereignty is rooted in the people, it is to be tempered by the law and respect for principles embedded in the U.S. Constitution.

For democratic action to reflect and advance the values of the republic, and for the collective body of Americans to bring this aspiration to life, it takes *thinking* like a democratic citizen. In this chapter, I grapple with tensions in thought and the gaps between how we conceive of American democracy and how we practice it. This chapter also offers an assertion that acknowledging these tensions and looking at this democratic experiment honestly and critically is just the sort of "well considered patriotism" that Tocqueville identified in Americans in the early 1800s, and is just the sort of patriotism required of the nation today.

What Is a "Democratic Sensibility" and Why Does It Matter?

Engaged citizenship is multifaceted and includes not just widely acknowledged forms of democratic participation such as voting, but a multitude of other actions meant to hold elected representatives accountable. A considerable amount of scholarship in recent years has advanced a framework of engaged democratic citizenship that consists of multiple dimensions, often overlapping with each other. Broad in scope, this umbrella-like view of engagement includes "any activity, individual or collective, devoted to influencing the life of the polity."[2] The wide spectrum of activities considered engagement, then, would include acquiring political knowledge, expressing your political voice, talking to others about politics, voting, and non-electoral activities from attending informational forums about an issue to joining a volunteer or community group.[3] A similar definition conceptualizes civic engagement as "developing knowledge about the community . . . , identifying and seeking solutions to community problems, pursuing goals to benefit the community, ... constructive deliberation among community members," and "actively participating in and seeking to influence the life of the community."[4] Activities such as gathering and sharing information, voting and participating in voter registration drives, advancing a petition, being involved in civic and political associations, attending meetings or public protests, and even being involved in the discussion of community and/or political issues, whether they are held in private or in public forums, all would be characterized as types of democratic involvement.[5]

Similarly, civic preparedness is multifaceted and amounts to more than possessing political knowledge. Civic competency also entails being equipped with the skills and the disposition to be democratic citizens.[6] For example, understanding how to watch a political debate critically or join with others to solve a community problem are skills necessary for active democratic participation. Additionally, possessing such democratic attitudes as a sense of civic responsibility or duty, or a belief that one has a role to play in democracy, further prepare us to be informed and engaged citizens.

Democratic action is about more than the action itself, then, but the ideals animating such action and such thinking go beyond knowing the ins and outs of American history or the intricacies of the Constitution. Judge Learned Hand, a judge on U.S. District Court for the Southern District of New York (1909–1924) and the U.S. Court of Appeals for the Second Circuit (1924–1961), expressed that American values, such as liberty, lie "in the hearts of men and women" and can be likened to a "spirit." "What then is the spirit of liberty? I cannot define it. I can only tell you my own faith. The spirit of liberty is the spirit which is not too sure that it is right, the spirit of liberty is the spirit that seeks to understand the mind of other men and women; the spirit of liberty is the spirit that weighs their interests alongside its own without bias."[7]

Similarly, Tocqueville remarked upon the democratic mindset he perceived among Americans. He wrote, "It is easy to see that the minds of almost all the inhabitants of the United States move in the same direction and are guided according to the same rules; that is to say, they possess, without ever having gone to the trouble of defining the rules, a certain philosophical methodology common to all of them."[8]

If democracy was a methodology for Tocqueville, it was a song for Walt Whitman. As he captures in his 1891 poem "I Hear America Singing," we hear this democratic song in the labor of the busy worker, "I Hear America singing, the varied carols I hear, / Those of mechanics, each one singing his as it should be blithe and strong." For Whitman, democracy is captured in the everyday actions of everyday people and convey the essential elements of democratic life: "Each singing what belongs to him or her and to none else, / The day what belongs to the day—at night, the party of young fellows, robust, friendly, / Singing with open mouths their strong melodious songs."

History is marked by examples of how a common appreciation for the promise of democracy's ideals has inspired and galvanized Americans. What else but a belief in the fundamental value of liberty would embolden tens of thousands of American troops, facing the certainty of grave casualties, to storm the beaches of Normandy on D-Day in 1944, precipitating the liberation of France from Nazi Germany and the end of World War II? What else but a belief in the fundamental value of equality would fortify John Lewis and other civil rights activists to cross the Edmund Pettus Bridge on March 7, 1965, a day that has become known as "Bloody Sunday," fully knowing that they would be blocked and likely physically attacked by Alabama state troopers?

In contrast, the consequences can be detrimental when the populace doesn't share a common democratic mindset. Although instigation by former President Trump and misinformation generated and spread via social media played a part in motivating thousands to storm the Capitol on January 6, 2021, it seems clear that participants' actions also were motivated that day by a perverted understanding of American democracy. *New York Times*' synchronized video footage of the day is marked with images of the American flag, recitations of the Pledge of Allegiance, and references to those storming the Capitol as "patriots." President Trump's daughter Ivanka even referred to participants as "American patriots" in a tweet that day that she later deleted.[9] As one participant in the "Stop the Steal" action explained, "it's so much more than just rallying for President Trump, it's really rallying for our way of life, the American dream."[10] Rather than antithetical to democratic expectations, storming the Capitol during the certification of the Electoral College vote seems to have been perceived by many as an exercise of freedom or an act of patriotism.

To be sure, Americans' enjoyment of democratic ideals varies considerably, with stark divides along income, ethnic, racial, and gender lines. Research has demonstrated that a person's civic identity or sense of connection to American democracy is influenced by their background and lived experience. In her research on young adults, Beth Rubin found that the civic identity of young adults is strongly related to the congruity (or lack thereof) that they perceive between their lived experiences and the ideals of American democracy they've been taught in school. For example, young people in her study who grew up in predominantly white, safe, and economically secure communities tended to see resonance between their lives and the foundational ideas contained in the Bill of Rights and Pledge of Allegiance. In contrast, many students, particularly those of color from low-income communities, saw real contrasts between their daily lives and core democratic tenets.[11]

While there are plenty of instances in which the nation has met the democratic ideal, there also are plenty of instances in which the democratic ideal is more aspirational than real. "Keeping the republic" requires understanding what that democratic ideal is and holding a common sensibility about the nation's democratic past, present, and future.

LIBERTY AND EQUALITY

What, then, are the tenets that animate democracy and really shape the way democratic citizens think? Although multifaceted, it's fair to say that American democratic thinking revolves around a shared commitment to the value of liberty. How we conceive of liberty varies in both theory and practice. Liberty can be understood as freedom *from* government intrusion, but it also can be seen as more positive in nature, with an innate commitment to foster conditions of liberty for others. However, American thought expects that liberty will flourish alongside equality. Although the value of equality also holds a range of expectations, it is clear that aspiring to achieve such equality remains an ongoing challenge but of equal importance to securing liberty.

Much of what most Americans understand about liberty and equality is gleaned from documents related to the American Revolutionary War and the years afterward—the Declaration of Independence, the U.S. Constitution, and the *Federalist Papers*. The *Federalist Papers* were a series of essays authored by Alexander Hamilton, John Jay, and James Madison (published under the pseudonym "Publius") meant to advocate for the ratification of the U.S. Constitution. It's worth acknowledging early in this exploration that benchmarks in the nation's history and even democratic thought are a function of choices made by historians, scholars, and "we the people," and that these choices have an impact on how we tell the story of American democracy. As Saladin Ambar argues, although we often look to the period of the 1770s and 1780s and the mid-Atlantic states as the time and location of the nation's beginning, the collective choice might have been made to date the founding closer to the arrival of the first settlers in the early 1600s and the arrival of the first ship of enslaved Africans in 1619 in Jamestown, Virginia.[12] By extension, our appreciation of American democratic values also is informed by the manner in which we've depicted the American experience—a depiction that often overlooks the glaring contradictions in the "truths we hold to be self-evident" and to whom these truths have applied.

In the often-cited *Federalist* No. 10, Madison asserts that the representative form of government proposed at the Constitutional Convention offers the greatest protection against the encroachment of government on the liberty of the individual, and that such preservation is of paramount importance. Madison and the other authors of the *Federalist Papers* characterized liberty as a natural-born right, one endowed by God and not the state. As Madison explains, this liberty might be manifested as "A zeal for different opinions concerning religion, concerning government, and many other points as well of speculation as of practice."[13]

It is fair to say that the vision of liberty found in the *Federalist Papers* characterizes the natural right of liberty as a "negative" right—one that must be protected from government intrusion. This notion stands in contrast to such political philosophers as Jean-Jacques Rousseau and the sort of government proposed in his book *The Social Contract*—one that regards the "general will" as a centerpiece and envisions citizens gaining social or positive rights by virtue of their social contract with government.

The American notion of the social contract seems more in line with English philosopher John Locke's view that the role of government is to protect one's self-interest. Because humans are rational, Locke holds that individuals determined that it made good sense to emerge out of the "state of nature" and engage in a contract with those selected to serve in government. In exchange for obeying the laws devised and enforced by government, government would protect the individual's self-interest and our natural rights, which are those rights one possesses by virtue of being human. Here, then, the role and purpose of government is limited—a tone set in the Declaration of Independence: "We hold these Truths to be self-evident, that all men are created equal, that all are endowed by their Creator with certain inalienable Rights, that among these are Life, Liberty, and the Pursuit of Happiness. That to secure these Rights, Governments are instituted among Men, deriving their just powers from the consent of the Governed, that whenever any Form of Government becomes destructive of these Ends, it is the Right of the People to alter or to abolish it, and to institute new Government."

Part and parcel, then, in the prominence of liberty as a founding belief was the notion that governmental power was to be regarded with suspicion and care, and that expansive governmental power posed a threat to this fundamental value. The danger in emphasizing the central role of liberty and the ancillary concern about governmental intrusion is that *freedom of the individual* often is understood as taking precedence over the good of the community as a whole, or as superior to other democratic values such as equality. Although much of American thought is motivated by preserving the individual's freedom, reducing our understanding of democratic thinking to this singular version of freedom ignores its truly expansive quality. Indeed, thinking like a democratic citizen entails a recognition that freedom can only be realized in a system that ensures equality, and that such freedom is enjoyed in the context of community. Not all necessarily agree with this idea. The relationship between the values of liberty and equality has received considerable attention among political theorists and scholars, with some arguing that liberty only is possible with equality and others asserting, even lamenting, that there is inherent tension between the two.

Contemporary scholar Danielle Allen makes a convincing argument that liberty and equality are not mutually exclusive ideals—neither in ancient political thought nor in the less ancient Declaration of Independence. In an essay for the *Washington Post*, Allen asserted that ancient Athens and ancient Rome formulated the ideas of "equality before the law" and devised "mixed" political systems that allowed for a balance of equality and liberty; "equality and liberty were concepts understood to support and sustain each other. Bonds of political and social equality among the citizens were necessary to forge institutions that would protect each individually from domination by the others and all together from domination by external powers."[14] As Allen points out, it was Abraham Lincoln who described the United States as "conceived in liberty and dedicated to the proposition that all men are created equal."

It was the backlash to the rise of Marxism in the mid-1800s, she argues, that has fueled the sense that these are oppositional values, or at least in competition with one another. The body of thought originating with Karl Marx, in which the working class or "proletariat" assumes the role of ruling class, prioritizes egalitarianism, and regards capitalism as antithetical to the individual's humanity and freedom itself. Indeed, it is by socializing the instruments used to produce goods that true freedom is realized. The spread of communism and its offshoots in the late 1800s and 1900s, and the resulting Cold War, sparked a response by political economists in defense of capitalism. This response advanced the idea that liberty and equality are not interwoven and that the sort of equality envisioned in Marxist thought amounted to an infringement of liberty, and therefore was antithetical to the essence of democracy. This sentiment is captured well by prominent political economist Milton Freidman, who wrote, "A society that puts equality . . . ahead of freedom will end up with neither equality or freedom. . . . On the other hand, a society that puts freedom first will, as a happy by-product, end up with greater freedom and greater equality."[15]

Others, who may have been sympathetic to the idea of actively fostering a system of egalitarianism, also questioned whether liberty and equality could coexist. For example, philosopher Isaiah Berlin's work explores the tensions between liberty, "value pluralism," and equality, holding that humans possess fundamental values that, although innate, may conflict with others (in contrast to "monism" or a sort of moral absolutism). Freely living according to these sometimes conflicting values may not only disrupt the balance between freedom and equality, it may make it impossible for the ideals to coexist.[16]

"We hold these Truths to be self-evident, that all men are created equal, that all are endowed by their Creator with certain inalienable Rights, that among these are Life, Liberty, and the Pursuit of Happiness." It is worth repeating this line of the

Declaration of Independence—like the inherent value of freedom, equality is a self-evident truth. Of course, we shouldn't
overlook the fact that the equality the Framers envisioned (and
liberty, for that matter) was limited to white, property-holding
men. Still, the value of equality holds just as much prominence
and importance as liberty.

Looking to the Declaration of Independence as her primary
source, Danielle Allen writes, "Political philosophers have generated the view that equality and freedom are necessarily in
tension with each other. As a public, we have swallowed this
argument whole. We think we are required to choose between
freedom and equality. . . . Such a choice is dangerous. If we
abandon equality, we lose the single bond that makes us a community, that makes us a people with the capacity to be free
collectively and individually in the first place."[17]

Indeed, according to Allen, the ideals are reliant upon each
other. "Equality is the foundation of freedom because from a
commitment to equality emerges the people itself—we, the
people—with the power both to create a shared world in which
all can flourish and to defend it from encroachers."[18]

Approaching the mutual dependence from another angle,
Jennifer Victor conceptualizes democracy as a personal trait
as well as a governmental trait. She asserts that the healthiest
democracies are those that not only recognize the centrality
of both freedom and equality but vigilantly work to balance
them within the individual and in the collective practice of
politics. "Another way to think about democracy is that it is
not just an adjective that describes the complementary and
competing ideals of freedom and equality with regard to gov-

ernment, but that democracy describes how much each individual person has its traits. In other words, democracy is not something given to everyone equally. It doesn't describe the state of government or society around us; rather, it describes the relative level of freedom and equality that each of us has as individuals, and it varies among us."[19]

At the individual level, one's sense of freedom or liberty is a function of how fairly he or she is treated in society and how equitable their access is to such public goods as education, health care, and safety, according to Victor. When larger and larger numbers of citizens possess declining levels of freedom and equality, democracy collectively suffers, and it takes the collective of democratic citizens to see to each individual's enjoyment of liberty and equality.

Democratic thinking, then, surely can recognize liberty as a fundamental theme in the American story without declaring it the only theme, nor necessarily the most dominant one. Instead, liberty can be thought of both individually and in the context of the community. Although an essential element of American democratic thought, liberty has a complexity that often is not fully appreciated but deserves to be. In response to the constitutional monarchy they left, the Framers certainly envisioned the value as "freedom from" governmental intrusion. Could such an outlook be tempered by a recognition that the universal enjoyment of this freedom required commensurate attention to the good of the community and the innate equality of members of this community? Such a multifaceted conception of liberty not only allows for the enjoyment of one's rights; it offers a setting conducive to the representative form

Figure 2.   Declaration of Independence. Courtesy of the
National Archives.

of government the Framers of the Constitution sought to put
into place.

Individuality and Unity

Since its early days, the phrase "e pluribus unum" (out of many,
one) traditionally has served as the United States' motto and

appears on such official symbols as the nation's Great Seal and coins minted by the U.S. Treasury. As foundational as liberty and equality, "out of many, one" evokes the nation's dual commitment to both the exercise and enjoyment of individuality and the common good that emerges from the exercise of such freedom. Best characterized as pluralistic in nature, the notion of balancing individuality with unity serves as the underpinning of the nation's governmental structure. Of course, theorizing American democracy as a cacophony of diverse notes that ultimately comes together in a beautiful symphony is an ideal worth striving toward but not always achieved in practice.

As the authors of the *Federalist Papers* saw it, a natural result of a free society centered around protection of liberty are "factions." Madison's conception of a faction is akin to our current understanding of an interest group or an organized interest: "a number of citizens, whether amounting to a majority or minority of the whole, who are united and actuated by some common impulse of passion, or of interest, adverse to the rights of other citizens, or to the permanent and aggregate interests of the community."[20]

Although an offshoot of the natural right of liberty, the challenges associated with these divisions was clear. Characterizing them as a "dangerous vice," Madison warned that factions introduce "instability, injustice, and confusion" and that "the public good is disregarded in the conflicts of rival parties."[21] The quandary, then, was what do about the resulting "mischiefs" associated with these factions. To squash the freedom that causes divisions or factions is to destroy the association of citizens itself. "Liberty is to faction as air is to fire, an aliment without which it instantly expires. But it could not be a less folly to abolish liberty, which is essential to political life, because it nourishes faction than it would be to wish the annihilation of air, which is essential to animal life, because it imparts to fire its destructive agency."[22]

Curing the "mischiefs" that factions promote by instilling a common set of beliefs or opinions not only would be impractical, it also would undermine the core tenet of preserving liberty. The only way to address the challenges associated with liberty, then, was to manage their effects, and the best way to manage their effects was through governmental design—a pluralist design that would foster compromise.

It is in *Federalist* No. 51 that we gain a sense of the rationale in structuring a system in which power is separated in numerous ways—legislative, executive, and judicial powers are three separate but equal branches; the legislative body is bicameral, with a Senate and a House of Representatives; and the governmental system is federal in nature, with national and state powers delineated. The reasoning behind such a form of government in which power was separated and the power exerted by some could be checked by others was that it offered the best remedy for preserving freedom while controlling for its effects. By constructing a form of government in which "ambition must be made to counter ambition," as Madison argued in *Federalist* No. 51, government's ability (and even inclination) to encroach upon the liberty of the citizen would be thwarted.

Cumbersome and complicated as it may be, a governmental system based on competition between branches and levels of government and even factions of the citizenry was the best safeguard to liberty in the opinion of the Framers, offering the "greatest security against a gradual concentration of the several powers in the same department."[23] Moreover, such a governmental structure that fostered the competition of interests theoretically also would foster collaborations or compromises that ultimately would reflect the will of the populace. For example, a system that allows the U.S. Congress to override a presidential veto if two-thirds of the members voting in the House and the Senate agree to do so might prompt compromise between representatives in order to achieve the veto override.

We conceive of the functioning of government, then, as the free but synthesized exercise of a diverse set of interests filtered through a governmental system of separated but balanced powers. Such a conceptualization relies on a few core assumptions, of course—that all interests or factions are able to form and represent themselves equally, that power is distributed and exercised equally among the branches of government, and that the actions of those serving in government are motivated primarily by their affiliation with the body they serve rather than their political party or themselves. The theory and practice of politics have shown that these assumptions don't always hold true—themes that will be touched upon throughout this text.

A good deal of political science research has explored the contours of American pluralism. Some have examined pluralism *empirically* to determine the degree to which pluralism explains politics, while others have looked at American pluralism *normatively* to establish what is most appropriate in a system such as the United States'.[24] The unity that can be achieved via this organized system of competition is an ongoing consideration. An additional feature of the America's democratic system that is meant to provide cohesion is a federal Constitution and the rule of law. It is the umbrella under which this competition of interests and system of checks and balances transpires. The ballast the Constitution provides against not only "ambition countering ambition," but the power of the majority, which is where we turn our attention next.

Majority Rule and Minority Rights

A third set of values or democratic principles that are seemingly contradictory but are meant to work in tandem is a commitment both to supporting and enabling the wishes of the populace while preserving the rights of those not in the majority but in the minority. It makes sense, of course, that a democratic form of government is rooted in the will of the people, or majority rule. Exercising that will without trampling on the inherent rights of the minority has been the ongoing challenge—a challenge ideally met with a shared commitment to the rule of law and the supremacy of the principles embedded in the Constitution.

Although committed to a popular form of government, or a government that was legitimized by "the people," there were concerns about the shortcomings of a *pure* democracy. Of greatest concern was the threat involved when a faction consisted of a majority of the populace. In such a circumstance, both the public good and the rights of individuals are threatened by the "ruling passion."[25] For those constructing the Constitution, finding a way to mitigate the potential for injustice or loss of rights when a faction is made up of a majority of the populace without undermining the liberty of such a faction to form was the problem in search of a solution. A representative or republican form of government offered such a solution. By setting up a system of representation, the authors of the *Federalist Papers* asserted that those selected to represent the populace would filter or modulate the passions of the majority and see to the good of the nation as a whole. As Madison explains, the effect of such a system will be "to refine and enlarge the public views by passing them through the medium of a chosen body of citizens, whose wisdom might best discern the true interest of their country and whose patriotism and love of justice will be least likely to sacrifice it to temporary or partial considerations."[26]

Even more, the bustle or competition of interests built into a republican form of government with powers separated and a system of checks and balances was a way to keep the majority from gaining too much power and undermining those in the minority. As Madison explains, "In the extended republic of the United States, and among the great variety of interests, parties, and sects which it embraces, a coalition of a majority of the whole society could seldom take place on any other principles than those of justice and the general good."[27]

The fundamental safeguard meant to ensure the rights of the minority and the principles embedded in the nation's democratic system of government is the Constitution of the United States. Indeed, the United States is not only a representative democracy, it's a constitutional democracy.[28] Signed on September 17, 1787, at the Pennsylvania State House (now known as Independence Hall), the Constitution establishes the structure and organization of the nation's governmental system, stipulates the relative powers of each branch of government, and describes the relationship of the states to the federal government.[29] Not only does the Constitution outline how the government will operate, it articulates via a Bill of Rights the fundamental rights of the citizen and the limitations of the government. Essential to the ratification of the Constitution, the Bill of Rights specifies the rights of Americans and aims to guarantee such civil rights and liberties as freedom of speech, the right to assemble, freedom of the press and of religion, and to protect these fundamental rights from government encroachment. Here, then, at least in theory but not always in practice throughout the life of the republic, the essential rights of the minority are meant to be safeguarded even in the face of the will of the majority.

It is the Constitution, then, that is meant to act as the counterweight to the will of the majority and to serve as the protector of the rights of the minority. Moreover, such Supreme Court cases as *Marbury v. Madison* and *McCulloch v. Maryland* have positioned the Constitution and the decisions rendered by the Supreme Court as the supreme law of the land—the final word on what is in keeping with the spirit of American democracy and what isn't. Indeed, it is to the Constitution that public officials, such as the president and members of Congress, swear their allegiance—not to a political party, or a single individual, or even "we the people."

Like all of the values articulated above, fidelity to constitutional principles has been practiced imperfectly throughout America's history and certainly up to the present day. It is also worth highlighting that filtering the "ruling passion" entailed minimizing the voices and the agency of all those that did not possess the power of the white, free men who owned property, thereby serving as an effective safeguard to maintain the power of those creating the republic's new form of government. Indeed, James Madison himself, the man who put many of these democratic ideals into print, relied upon an extensive number of enslaved men and women to maintain his estate, Montpelier, in Virginia and during his presidency.[30]

The nation's system of representation and other original measures used to check the power of the majority, such as the Electoral College and Senate confirmation of lifetime judicial appointees, have had enduring effects on the ability of the majority to exercise their will and shape the direction of government action. On this note, David Frum, former speechwriter for President George W. Bush, writes in exploring the shortcomings of the Founders' constitutional design, "The system of government in the United States has evolved in many important ways since 1787. But the mistrust of unpropertied majorities—especially urban unpropertied majorities—persists."[31] Indeed, citizens' ability to exercise their power has led some scholars to question how democratic American

democracy actually is. For example, Sanford Levinson points
to such features as the lifetime appointments of Supreme Court
justices and the presidential veto power as antithetical to
democracy and has argued that the nation needs a contemporary Constitutional Convention to address the system's
inadequacies. As it stands, the existing governmental system
is inadequate, according to Levinson. "Serious liberals and
conservatives would likely disagree on the particular failings,
but both, increasingly, would share an attitude of profound
disquiet about the capacity of our institutions to meet the
problems confronting us as a society."[32]

LINKING THEORY WITH PRACTICE

In July of 1974, the House Judiciary Committee met to determine whether the House of Representatives should adopt
articles of impeachment against Richard Nixon for his
involvement in the break-in at the Democratic Party offices in
the Watergate building and the subsequent cover-up. Representing Texas, Barbara Jordan was the first African American
woman in the twentieth century elected to Congress from the
Deep South, and she received a seat on the prestigious Judiciary Committee during her first term in Congress.[33] A gifted
orator, Jordan's opening remarks at the impeachment hearings
were gripping:

Earlier today, we heard the beginning of the Preamble to
the Constitution of the United States: "We, the people." It's
a very eloquent beginning. But when that document was

completed on the seventeenth of September in 1787, I was not included in that "We, the people." I felt somehow for many years that George Washington and Alexander Hamilton just left me out by mistake. But through the process of amendment, interpretation, and court decision, I have finally been included in "We, the people."

Today I am an inquisitor. An hyperbole would not be fictional and would not overstate the solemnness that I feel right now. My faith in the Constitution is whole; it is complete; it is total. And I am not going to sit here and be an idle spectator to the diminution, the subversion, the destruction, of the Constitution.[34]

Jordan's quote reflects the exercise of thinking like a democratic citizen in the United States. Not only do some of the core ideals seem incongruous, so much of the American experience and the functioning of the nation's democracy seem at odds with the ideal. And yet, as Jordan references, it is a higher faith in the ideal that propels us. In just the same way the U.S. Constitution can be conceived as a "living document," it is fair to conceive of a democratic way of thinking as "aspirational." Although American history, past and present, often falls far short of the democratic ideals upon which it was based, they serve to inform the practice of democracy today and into the future. If liberty, equality, diversity, unity, popular sovereignty, and rule of law are the fundamental principles underpinning what it means to think like a democratic citizen, what does this thinking look like in practice? Are Americans today thinking like democratic citizens?

Figure 3. Barbara Jordan, member of the United States House
of Representatives. Source: Public domain.

Survey data suggest that, at least in the aggregate and at
least in theory, there seems to be support for the values articulated above. What is striking in contemporary politics,
though, is how partisanship cuts through Americans' collective support for these values. Of course, *thinking* our way out
of democratic challenges is not always possible—often, it's the

actual structure of American government and its historical underpinnings that make it difficult for these values to be made real.

In their 2018 survey of Americans' views on the nation's democratic ideals and values, the Pew Research Center found general agreement among respondents on what were the most important democratic values, many of which align with those democratic principles explored in this chapter. For instance, a majority of those surveyed indicated that it was very important for the country that "rights and freedoms of all people are respected" (84%), "judges are not influenced by political parties" (82%), "everyone has an equal opportunity to succeed" (82%), "Republicans and Democrats work together on issues" (78%), "balance of power between government branches" (76%), "people are free to peacefully protest" (74%), "views of those not in the majority on issues are respected" (62%).[35]

For the most part, the Pew survey found broad acceptance, regardless of political party affiliation, of these values. For example, relatively large and commensurate shares of Republican and Democratic respondents agreed that it's very important that "elected officials face serious consequences for misconduct" and that "news organizations are independent of government." There were some notable partisan differences, though. The importance of the right to protest varied by party, with 82 percent of those who lean Democratic saying it is very important that "people are free to peacefully protest" compared with 64 percent of those who lean Republican.[36] Assessments of how well the nation lives up to these values is also where variance between parties was most notable. The Pew survey found, for example, that 74 percent of Republicans and those who leaned Republican believed the phrase "everyone has an equal opportunity to succeed" described the country well, compared to 37 percent of Democrats and those who lean Democratic. Similarly, 60 percent of those aligning with the Republican Party thought the phrase "the rights and freedoms of all people are respected" accurately represented the nation today, compared 38 percent of Democrats.[37]

As political scientist Larry Bartels has pointed out in recent research regarding the relationship between partisanship and democratic commitment, social scientists have struggled for years to discern the populace's fidelity to democratic ideals when presented in the abstract compared to their commitment to living up to these values in reality. As Bartels notes, Prothro and Griggs' 1960 research found that majorities of survey respondents endorsed "the basic principles of democracy when they are put in abstract terms," but that "consensus breaks down completely" when "broad principles are translated into more specific propositions."[38]

Similarly, scholars have sought to better understand the role of partisanship in the degree and nature of democratic commitment, especially when respondents are pressed to envision putting these practices into practice. Research by Feierherd, Lupu, and Stokes conducted in 2017 (with a Republican serving as president) found that Republicans were twice as likely as Democrats (24%–11%) to hold that "when the country is facing very difficult times it is justifiable for the president of the country to close the Congress and govern without Congress."

Notably, results were reversed in 2014 when the White House was controlled by a Democrat—more Democrats than Republicans (30%–6%) were comfortable with the president closing Congress and governing in its place.[39]

Although both parties demonstrate a willingness to jettison democratic ideals when pressed to apply them in real life, scholars continue to grapple with the foundation on which this willingness is based and to discern whether these bases vary between parties. Bartels's research leads him to conclude that antidemocratic tendencies are not a function of social isolation, limited education, or lack of political interest. Situating his research in the context of the Trump presidency and the Republican Party, Bartels concludes that, among Republican respondents, these tendencies can be explained by "real political values—specifically, and overwhelmingly, in Republicans' ethnocentric concerns about the political and social role of immigrants, African-Americans, and Latinos in a context of significant demographic and cultural change."[40]

Concerns about partisan polarization and the ideological direction of the Republican Party predate the presidency of Donald Trump. In their analysis of the functioning (or malfunctioning) of Congress and the political process as a whole, ideological counterparts Thomas Mann and Norman Ornstein (Mann from the Brookings Institution and Ornstein from the American Enterprise Institute) cite the detrimental role partisanship has played in the operation of government in recent history. They assert that, although it is not singularly responsible, asymmetric partisan polarization has played a significant role in government's ability to function effectively, declaring that the Republican Party has become "ideologically extreme; contemptuous of the inherited social and economic policy regime; scornful of compromise; unpersuaded by conventional understanding of facts, evidence, and science; and dismissive of the legitimacy of its political opposition."[41]

Such declarations aren't reserved to scholars and political analysts. Prominent public officials who represented the Republican Party while serving in office have decried the state of the party they once represented. In a *Washington Post* op-ed announcing the creation of "A Call for American Renewal," a nationwide rallying cry against extremist elements within the GOP, former public officials Charlie Dent, Mary Peters, Denver Riggleman, Michael Steele, and Christine Todd Whitman[42] write, "Tragically, the Republican Party has lost its way, perverted by fear, lies and self-interest. What's more, GOP attacks on the integrity of our elections and our institutions pose a continuing and material threat to the nation."[43] Some of the core principles of "A Call for American Renewal" include ideas discussed earlier in this chapter—"democracy," "founding ideals," "constitutional order," "rule of law," "pluralism," and "free speech."[44]

Partisanship undercuts democratic thinking in other ways, making it more difficult to achieve what one might expect in a democracy. Survey data from the Pew Research Center highlights how intense partisanship among Americans extends beyond a person's partisan affiliation to their personal attributes. A majority of Republican respondents labeled Democrats as immoral (an increase of 8% from three years earlier) and 63 percent held that, compared with other Americans,

Democrats are "more unpatriotic." On the other side of the aisle, 47 percent of Democrats said that Republican were immoral compared to other Americans (an increase of 12% since 2016), and 75 percent characterized Republicans as closed-minded.[45] Clearly, these sentiments stand in contrast to the ideals enumerated earlier.

Scholars, analysts, and public servants continue to grapple with how Americans today think of democratic citizenship, what factors influence this thinking, and the role this sort of thinking holds in the conduct of politics. Again, democratic mindsets can't solely explain why the nation's democratic promise doesn't always deliver. As noted earlier in this chapter, historical and institutional factors often make it challenging, if not impossible, to meet the ideal. Although the entrenched partisanship of American politics can be attributed to such factors as campaign finance or gerrymandering, it's worth noting that the dominance of the two-party system in the United States is rooted in the structure of the nation's governmental system. Unlike parliamentary systems, representation in the U.S. Congress is determined by a "winner take all" electoral system within single-member districts—a system in which there is little benefit or incentive for smaller parties to organize. In parliamentary systems, smaller parties that secure fewer votes are granted at least some representation in their legislative bodies. This has come to be known as "Duverger's law," a political science theory that holds that the plurality rule for selecting the winner of elections favors a two-party system.[46] The United States' two-party system, then, a system currently mired in ill will, is a function of the structural nature of the United States' governing system. Here is just one example of the aspirations of American democracy bumping up against the nuts and bolts of American democracy—often democratic ideals (such as compromise in this instance) can't be realized if the system is set up in such a way that the ideal is actually undermined.

Thinking Like a Democratic Citizen

Upon reflection of the United States, Tocqueville asserted that in order to persist, the connection of the people to the nation must move beyond "instinctive patriotism" and toward a "well-considered" brand of patriotism.[47] "Instinctive" patriotism is reverential in nature, stemming from an impulse of sentiment and expressed through devotion to ancient customs and traditions. For Tocqueville, this sort of "waving of the flag" patriotism, often directed at a monarch, is ephemeral.[48] The second sort of patriotism Tocqueville describes is more thoughtful in nature, not quite as ardent but "more creative and more lasting."[49] This more rational form of patriotism is innate in republican forms of government that value the rule of law. The strength of such democracies comes from the interconnection between the well-being of the political system and the well-being of the citizen. Witnessing American democracy in action in the 1830s, Tocqueville found that rooting the public spirit in shared political rights rather than simply in the land or customs or leaders resulted in a strong civic ethos and democratic stability.

My premise in this chapter is that the nation's collective mindset sets the foundation for democratic action. Although American democratic thought is complex and sometimes even contradictory, there are dangers to opting for a one-dimensional or "instinctive" sort of patriotism. A more lasting sort of democratic spirit comes with a willingness to recognize and grapple with the tensions not only in thought but in their practice today and throughout American history. In the remainder of this book, I will explore how our conceptions of democracy often do manifest in our practices . . . in how we talk about politics, organize elections, express our political opinion, and participate in our communities. There is value, then, in both celebrating the nation's democratic successes but also in calling out and seeking to rectify when we've fallen short.

Like Whitman in "I Hear America Singing," Langston Hughes's "Let America Be America Again" also celebrates the individual. If the everyday actions of everyday people conveyed the essential elements of democratic life for Whitman, though, they reflect the unfulfilled promise of the democratic experiment for Hughes:

> Let America be America again.
> Let it be the dream it used to be.
> Let it be the pioneer on the plain
> Seeking a home where he himself is free.
> (America never was America to me.)

In line with Barbara Jordan's worry "that George Washington and Alexander Hamilton just left me out by mistake,"

Hughes's powerful poem delineates the ways in which the American dream hasn't turned out to the be "the dream the dreamers dreamed," writing

> I am the poor white, fooled and pushed apart,
> I am the Negro bearing slavery's scars.
> I am the red man driven from the land.

As Hughes's conclusion suggests, it is in acknowledging and reckoning with the disjunctures in democratic thought and shortcomings in how it has been practiced that we get closer to the sort of democratic way of thinking that can handle the tensions between liberty and equality, between diversity and unity, between popular rule and the rule of law. Rooted in reason and not passion or instinct.

> O, yes,
> I say it plain,
> America never was America to me,
> And yet I swear this oath—
> America will be!

CHAPTER 3

Talking Like a
Democratic Citizen

In recent years, the deaths of prominent public officials with
long records of service have brought together a bipartisan mix
to honor them at public (often televised) funerals. From President George H. W. Bush, to Senator John McCain, to General
Colin Powell, these public servants have brought Republicans
and Democrats alike to mourn not only the person but a seemingly mythical time when people in public life got along and
put country over political party. This sentiment is clear in President Barack Obama's eulogy to Senator Jon McCain—his
opponent in the 2008 election for president:

> Now, in fact, John was a pretty conservative guy. Trust me:
> I was on the receiving end of some of those votes. But he
> did understand that some principles transcend politics,
> that some values transcend party. He considered it part of
> his duty to uphold those principles and uphold those val-
> ues. John cared about the institutions of self-government,
> our Constitution, our Bill of Rights, rule of law, separation

of powers, even the arcane rules and procedures of the Senate. He knew that in a nation as big and boisterous and diverse as ours, those institutions, those rules, those norms are what bind us together. They give shape and order to our common life, even when we disagree. Especially when we disagree. John believed in honest argument and hearing other views. He understood that if we get in the habit of bending the truth to suit political expediency or party orthodoxy, our democracy will not work.[1]

Harkening back to a time in which public officials got along is partly myth, of course—we surely can find examples not just of ugly discourse but also discourse that has led to violence throughout the nation's political history. These sentiments also ignore the systemic ugliness of excluding women, African Americans, and others from the public sphere for much of the nation's history. Myth or not, though, public responses to the passing of these figures reflect a pervasive disgust or dismay with the way in which we relate to one another.

If American democracy has the multifaceted or even abundant nature that Walt Whitman envisioned, then our collective democratic thinking can manifest itself in a variety of forms. Elements of democratic thinking might be recognizable in the way we organize government, our process of voting, the constituent services delivered by local elected officials, or other formal and tangible outgrowths of a republican form of government. Democratic thinking can permeate informal features of society as well, though—civic life, the arts, and culture. Indeed, the manner in which we relate to one another is a reflection of our thinking as democratic citizens.

Numerous indicators tell us that Americans' ability to relate to one another—to talk to each other—is in an unhealthy state. Examples abound of hateful and toxic speech—not only among elected officials but also among the public. Although differences of opinion are to be expected in a democracy that values liberty and diversity, Americans today express discomfort and an unwillingness to engage in discussions with those who disagree with them. The prevalence of social media along with challenges associated with discerning (and accepting) fact from fiction only amplify the vitriol of political discussions, driving people further apart. It's not as if such toxicity in our discourse is entirely new. Today, though, this toxicity has extended its reach and permeated our democratic practices.

This chapter explores the link between discourse and democracy and asserts that talking to each other about politics is a facet of democratic citizenship. Just like voting and holding elected officials accountable for their actions, democratic citizenship entails a willingness and a facility with engaging in political discussion. As this chapter will show, the challenges of talking politics today are being felt from the halls of power, to the classroom, to the kitchen table. At the same time, research and practice are identifying elements that foster productive political discourse and tools for equipping us to engage in such political conversation. Often, calls for elevating political discourse are offered as a call for "civility"—a notion that can serve to silence challenging or even threatening

speech or ideas. Equally problematic is the notion that freedom of speech must be unfettered in all settings—offering a
license to dehumanize and spread false information. Seeking
a balance, then, between free (and sometimes even loud and
angry) speech with a sense of equality and community must
be part of the consideration, the research, and the practice of
talking politics.

This chapter highlights some of this research and the best
practices that are emerging. If believing in liberty is fundamental to this American way of thought, then so is believing
that differences of opinion and debate are intrinsic to the
American experience. Without such a democratic spirit, we are
tempted to view disagreement not as an extension of our belief
in liberty but as wrong, unpatriotic, or even un-American. The
aim in this chapter is to call attention to the importance of
productive political discourse as a way to "keep the republic,"
encouraging and even enabling all of us to have the difficult
but necessary conversations self-government requires.

THE STATE OF POLITICAL DISCOURSE

Americans are disgusted by the current state of discourse, view
the acceptable boundaries of discourse differently based on
their political party, and find engaging in political discussion
stressful and unproductive. The Pew Research Center found
that most Americans are critical of the state of political discourse, asserting that the political debate has become "less
respectful, fact-based, and substantive."[2] The survey data show
that Americans aren't always clear on what is acceptable speech

and that Republicans are less likely than Democrats to feel comfortable expressing their opinion.[3] Just having political conversations with people with whom we disagree is increasingly viewed as stressful—59 percent of those surveyed in 2021 indicated that having political conversations with those they disagree with is "stressful and frustrating," an increase of 9 percent from data gathered two years earlier.[4]

Discourse among Public Officials

These popular sentiments are not altogether surprising given the tenor of American politics in recent years—public discourse marked by the sort of disrespectful and combative language Americans profess to find stressful and inappropriate. This vitriol has been evident at the federal level of government but also has pervaded state and local government—including boards of education. To be sure, politics of the past were not free of vitriol or even violence. Heated debates in the 1850s regarding the issue of slavery, for instance, extended to the U.S. Congress when Representative Preston Brooks of South Carolina entered the Senate chamber on May 22, 1856, and repeatedly struck Senator Charles Sumner of Massachusetts over the head with a cane. The assault was in reaction to a speech in which Sumner criticized slavery and the senators who supported it.[5] In more recent history, the violence surrounding the Democratic National Convention in August of 1968 reminds us that combative political discourse is not a new phenomenon.[6]

Although the 2016 election often is regarded as ushering in a modern and negative shift in public discourse with the

SOUTHERN CHIVALRY — ARGUMENT versus CLUB'S.

Figure 4. The Caning of Charles Sumner. Courtesy of the New York Public Library.

campaign and election of Donald Trump, elements of toxic discourse were quite evident during the presidency of Barack Obama. When delivering a speech to a joint session of Congress regarding health care early in his presidency, Republican Congressman Joe Wilson from South Carolina broke protocol and shouted out "You lie" in response to Obama's denial that the proposed legislation would provide free health coverage for those without legal citizenship. Wilson later apologized, stating, "This evening, I let my emotions get the best of me when listening to the president's remarks regarding the coverage of illegal immigrants in the health care bill.... While I disagree with the president's statement, my comments were inappropriate and regrettable. I extend sincere apologies to the president for this lack of civility."[7] Indeed, the proposed health care legislation sparked heated exchanges across the country in town halls between constituents and elected officials, exchanges marked by screaming and insults.[8]

The campaign of Donald Trump, though, launched a new era of political discourse, punctuated not only by coarse language but language that was menacing and violent in nature and imbued with racial and ethnic hostility. The tone was set with a campaign launch that was less about inspiring the nation to reach its highest ideals than it was a litany of ways in which the nation was being beaten and exploited by other countries, or as Trump surmised, "The U.S. has become a dumping ground for everybody else's problems."[9] Equally damaging to discourse was the pervasive use of false and misleading claims by candidate and then President Trump. Over the course of his presidency, the *Washington Post* calculated that Trump made 30,573 false or misleading claims.[10] Of course, the former president's use of the platform formerly known as Twitter (with an estimated high of 80 million followers prior to his suspension from the platform in January 2021) provided an unprecedented megaphone.[11] It also made him a focal point for much of the blame for the state of political discourse, with a majority of the population asserting in a 2019 survey that Trump changed the tone of political debate in the United States for the worse.[12]

Space doesn't allow for a chronicle of the statements and tweets coming from the former president that exemplify this tone, or the responses by public officials in opposition to Trump—such as Speaker of the House Nancy Pelosi ripping the transcript of Trump's 2020 State of the Union speech from the rostrum. Characterizations, though, both by citizens and those in political power, of the January 6th attack on the Capitol meant to restore Trump to the White House offer a stark example of contrasting perceptions on the appropriate bounds of discourse. On February 4, 2022, the Republican National Committee censured Republican House members Liz Cheney and Adam Kinzinger for their involvement in investigations related to the events of January 6, 2021, asserting that their actions reflected disloyalty to former President Trump. "The Conference must not be sabotaged by Representatives Liz Cheney and Adam Kinzinger who have demonstrated, with actions and words, that they support Democrat efforts to destroy President Trump more than they support winning back a Republican majority in 2022." Most stunning in their censure was the characterization of events of that day as acceptable forms of speech. The censure reads, "Representatives Cheney and Kinzinger are participating in a Democrat-led persecution of ordinary citizens engaged in legitimate political discourse."[13]

Prominent Republican officeholders criticized the censure by the RNC. Senator Mitt Romney of Utah tweeted, "Shame falls on a party that would censure persons of conscience, who seek truth in the face of vitriol. Honor attaches to Liz Cheney and Adam Kinzinger for seeking truth even when doing so comes at great personal cost." The Republican governor of Maryland, Larry Hogan, tweeted, "The GOP I believe in is the party of freedom and truth. It's a sad day for my party—and the country—when you're punished just for expressing your beliefs, standing on principle, and refusing to tell blatant lies,"

Still, the RNC speaks for the Republican Party and this statement speaks volumes.

The last few years, then, have been marked by political discourse at various levels of government that not only is heated but has veered to threatening and dangerous. The global pandemic and efforts taken by public officials to combat it have only intensified these interactions. In a precursor to the events of January 6th, armed members of a Michigan militia occupied the state capitol building in the spring of 2020 as legislators were debating public health measures. The actions were part of "Unlock Michigan," an effort aimed at protesting Governor Gretchen Whitmer's coronavirus lockdown measures.[14] Boards of elections and boards of education haven't been immune from these sorts of protests, and also have been subjected to heated and even threatening comments—2022 research by Reuters of a sampling of school districts found 220 examples of local school officials threatened with violence and harassed with hostile (often anonymous) messages.[15]

Discourse on College Campuses

Questions regarding the boundaries of free speech and the contours of public discourse have not been restricted to the halls of government. The college campus has long been the context for such discussions, and the nature of the discussion has followed the conditions of the times. As Chemerinsky and Gillman write, "Controversies over freedom of speech on college campuses have existed as long as there have been college campuses. But the specific issues vary with each generation."[16] From student protests (sometimes violent) in reaction to speakers invited to campus, to calls for firings of professors for comments made on their social media platforms, to the "Unite the Right" rally at the University of Virginia at which participants shouted such racist and anti-Semitic statements as "Jews will not replace us," incidents in recent years have prompted a collective discussion about the nature of discourse on college campus.

The body of social science and legal scholarship and case law related to free speech on campus and academic freedom is too vast to be documented here. It is fair to say, though, that there has been a progression of thought on the function of higher education, the connection between education and the free exchange of ideas, and the responsibility of ensuring equity in academia and the academic experience. As Chemerinsky and Gillman chart, higher education began as a venue for teaching morality rather than intellectual inquiry. By the early 1900s, though, greater emphasis was placed on the role of the college campuses as serving as an incubator of ideas or a place of scholarly inquiry, with the American Association of University Professors publishing the "Declaration of Principles on Academic Freedom and Academic Tenure." With so many of the protest movements of the 1960s taking place on college campuses, higher education solidified itself as a location in which diverse and controversial issues could be debated and faculty could express their political opinion without fear of retribution.[17]

As campuses began to welcome a more diverse body of students, higher education also took steps to foster educational experiences and learning environments that were more inclusive of a range of students' lived experiences. As Nancy Thomas notes, with increases in minority student enrollment and more women entering college, campus culture and curriculums transformed—for example, more interdisciplinary programs such as women's studies and African American studies were offered; campuses began to create cultural centers and first-year experiences meant to bring diverse students together.[18] Over time, campus efforts to advance diversity, equity, and inclusion have become institutionalized. These efforts have sometimes been countered and tested at the campus level, in state legislatures, and even in federal law. Indeed, the question of how to foster campus environments that advance the values of academic freedom while also promoting a diverse and inclusive campus has devolved into a partisan debate. A 2018 Gallup–Knight Foundation study found that, although supportive of protecting expression on campuses, U.S. college students' views on expression and diversity varied according to political party—Republican students were more likely to favor protecting free speech rights and Democratic students were more likely to support promoting a diverse and inclusive society.[19]

The partisan nature of the topic of freedom of speech on college campuses has been reflected in the passage of campus free speech laws in a growing number of states[20] and even the issuance of an executive order by former President Trump threatening to deny campuses federal research money if they are not supportive of free speech.[21] In recent years, such legislative action has been extended to the elementary and high school classroom over concerns about the content of curriculum. PEN America noted a steep increase in 2022 of legislative proposals and the passage of state-level policy addressing what may be taught in classrooms from elementary schools through the college years, some of which impose harsh penalties.[22]

Talking Politics to Each Other

All of this has created the perception that we don't know how to (and don't really even want to) talk to each other about politics—a perception that even has led news outlets to publish guides on how to navigate heated political arguments at Thanksgiving dinners.[23] One opinion writer termed the phenomenon "Thanksgiving Derangement Syndrome"—an affliction for those spending Thanksgiving dinner with family members of opposing political beliefs. "Sufferers exhibit the following behaviors: Dread of Thanksgiving dinner with relatives from the other party, a tendency to drink too much and, most ominously, an uncontrollable compulsion to engage in bruising political arguments that make everybody present miserable, embittered, and in a hurry to leave. It's also easy to catch, and hard to control once a family is infected, and it afflicts partisans of both sides equally."[24]

The perception that Americans dread talking to each other, combined with survey data indicating that Americans are disgusted by the current state of discourse, view the acceptable boundaries of discourse differently based on their political party, and find engaging in political discussion stressful and unproductive, suggests the question: What does American democracy expect of its citizens when it comes to exchanging ideas and talking politics? How do we carry the seemingly contradictory ideals of freedom of speech and public good into our conversations—whether we're elected officials, classmates, or neighbors?

TALKING POLITICS AND DEMOCRATIC CITIZENSHIP

"Keeping the republic" requires more than formal and perhaps obvious democratic exercises such as voting; it also involves such informal behaviors as thinking like a democratic citizen and then carrying that thinking into our interactions with each other. Foundational to this idea, though, is the link between our civic awareness and self-government. Indeed, the job of the democratic citizen is not just to elect a body of representatives; it requires holding those representatives accountable, and we can only engage in that accountability if we are informed. What does it require to be informed? Identifying and consuming reliable information is a basic element, of course, but the exercise must also entail a willingness to challenge our own beliefs, entertain and test the ideas of others, and agree that truth be valued over fiction. This exercise must be vigorous and even can be confrontational and challenging, but guided by the understanding that democracy's social contract expects a balance between the ideals of diversity of ideas and common good, liberty and equality.

Being Informed

In his consideration of American democracy, Tocqueville noted an innate bustling and dynamism, writing, "No sooner do you set foot in America than you find yourself in sort of tumult; a confused clamor rises on every side; a thousand voices reach your ears at once, each expressing some social need."[25] For Tocqueville, this bustle resembled a sort of nosiness or need to be in the business of others and was an element of democratic society. "To have a hand in the government of society, and to talk about it, is the most important business and, so to speak, the only pleasure an American knows . . . if an American were to be reduced to minding his own business, he would be deprived of half his existence; he would experience it as a gaping void in his life and would become unbelievably unhappy."[26] For Tocqueville, it is this public attention that, messy as it may be, empowers democracies. "Democracy does not give its nation the most skillful administration but it ensures what the most skillful administration is often too powerless to create, namely to spread through the whole social community a restless activity, an overabundant force, an energy which never exists without it and which, however unfavorable the circumstances, can perform wonders. Therein lie its real advantages."[27]

In this spirit, then, democratic citizenship requires an engagement that is cognitive in nature, with the freedom and the reliable tools to be civically aware. In their study of engagement, Cliff Zukin and colleagues asserted that paying attention to politics can be both a precursor and an offshoot of other types of participation like voting and attending public meetings. This element of citizenship might involve watching the news, reading newspapers, following government or public affairs, and talking about politics with family and friends.[28]

There is evidence to support the link between civic awareness and other types of democratic action such as voting. As Peter Levine asserts, though, such awareness also allows us to "refine and test our general outlook and ideology. . . . Each significant news story helps us to revise and develop that worldview. In turn, our ideology shapes numerous consequential decisions: not only about federal elections, but also about where to live, what groups we join, and what we expect from schools."[29]

The links between education and the health and longevity of democracy have been asserted from early in the nation's founding to today. As Thomas Jefferson expressed in a letter to Charles Yancey in 1816, "if a nation expects to be ignorant & free, in a state of civilisation, it expects what never was & never will be. the functionaries of every government have propensities to command at will the liberty & property of their constituents. there is no safe deposit for these but with the people themselves; nor can they be safe with them without information. where the press is free and every man able to read, all is safe."[30] Some 200 years later, it was the National Task Force on Civic Learning and Engagement, a collaboration between the U.S. Department of Education and the American Association of Colleges and Universities, that asserted, "As a democracy, the United States depends on a knowledgeable, public-spirited, and engaged population."[31]

Having Difficult Conversations

Being informed requires consuming a diversity of ideas, grappling with them, and engaging in reasoned deliberation. Diana Hess makes a forceful case for the importance of discussion in *Controversy in the Classroom: The Democratic Power of Discussion*.[32] She argues that the talking and the listening that takes place in a political conversation reflects the essence of democracy—self-governance among equals. "The ideal of discussion supports the validity of intrinsic equality by implying, at least symbolically, that all members of a community are political equals and are therefore equally qualified to participate in discussion and decision-making."[33] Moreover, discussions that involve a diversity of viewpoints offer a route for building political tolerance across party lines and for learning—heightening the likelihood of better policies.[34] Indeed, the pluralism built into a democratic system in which ambition is meant to counter ambition (see *Federalist* No. 51) assumes a diversity of ideas and opinions—viewing such diversity as an offshoot of liberty. It also expects that out of this exchange of diverse views will come a compromise—a less than perfect but broadly agreed upon outcome.

Does political discussion come with other assumptions in a democratic republic? Specifically, what is the role of "civility" in political discussions and what do we mean by "civility"? In his introduction to the edited volume *A Crisis in Civility? Political Discourse and Its Discontents*, Robert Boatright asserts that the notion of civility in politics is a reflection of a civil society, or what "we have in common that precedes the establishment of political institutions. It assumes that when we define ourselves as a people, we do so by granting others within our groups a certain level of respect."[35] To urge civility is to promote a civil society—"a society in which there is a shared purpose, and in which citizens are capable of seeing their politics as a reflection of the people that have brought that politics into being ... moments of heightened incivility in our politics ... can serve as a reminder to us to pay closer attention to who we are as a people and to develop an inclusive, shared language about how we might solve our problems together."[36]

Philosopher Anthony Simon Laden argues that civility can be conceptualized in two ways. The first concept regards civility as a form of politeness or a set of manners that involves "not insulting those with whom you disagree, subjecting them to ad hominem arguments, or otherwise treating them rudely." The second conception is more responsive in nature and views civility as "a form of engagement in a shared political activity characterized by a certain kind of openness and disposition to cooperate ... a civic virtue that shapes the nature of our interactions with one another, and to what degree those interactions involve genuine responsiveness to one another."[37] For this second type of civility, action (or interaction to be more specific) is the defining feature.

How might these philosophical definitions be integrated into the practice of politics and political discussion? Certainly, we've seen many examples in recent years of violations of the conceptualization of civility as politeness, and as Landon argues, such incivility "coarsens public life and makes daily public interactions more stressful and less pleasant."[38] Conceiving of civility as a dynamic practice marked by a responsiveness to each other, though, is more in line with a version of democracy that values liberty and equality ... a diversity of views with an emphasis on coming together. Such an approach to discourse sees civility "as a cooperative virtue of political life," a "willingness to listen to each other," and a "fair-mindedness in considering their views and when one should adjust one's own position in response to theirs."[39] In this way, there is no great value in pure politeness as a form of civility if there is absolutely no intention of being open to others' views or no willingness to be moved by them. At the same time, there is certainly nothing wrong with being polite and mannerly when engaging in this sort of responsive civility—but being polite isn't necessarily the only goal.

Along these lines, some have warned that calls for "civility" often are a reaction by those benefiting from the status quo to the well-deserved anger and protest from marginalized communities who do not reap the same benefits. In defining one form of civility as politeness, Landon offers a similar concern: "While politeness can take the rough edges off of social interactions and thus make it easier, requirements of politeness can also serve to exclude members of certain groups from full participation in social life by setting out elaborate codes of conduct to which only some people are privy or by ruling out of court certain kinds of challenges to the status quo based purely on their manner of delivery."[40]

Indeed, the notion of "civility" might be viewed as an extension of efforts by whites to "civilize" Native Americans or enslaved Africans, and as scholar Gaye Theresa Johnson makes clear, "People of color don't get to orchestrate the terms of civility. . . . Instead, we're always responding to what civility is supposed to be." Reactions to protests such as Colin Kaepernick kneeling during the national anthem or the Black Lives Matter movement and calls for civility are informed by this need "to civilize," as political scientist and author of *Eloquent Rage: A Black Feminist Discovers Her Superpower* Brittney Cooper asserts. "Black anger, black rage, black distress over injustice is seen as, one, unreasonable and outsized; and, two, as a thing that must be neutralized and contained quickly."[41]

What the Scholarship Says

Out of the ever-growing body of scholarship on the topic of civility and its role in democracy, a few relevant findings are emerging. First, perceptions of what constitutes civil (or uncivil) discourse vary widely—among the public and among scholars. As Muddiman and Stroud claim, incivility often is "in the eye of the beholder."[42] Indeed, scholars' conception of civility and incivility may be at odds with the public's, hampering effective measurement and study.[43] Second, the public seems to have less tolerance for incivility in the form of a lack of politeness (such as name-calling or swearing) than incivility that manifests itself as a lack of responsiveness to other public servants or interactions that are devoid of the cooperative ethos outlined earlier. As Ashley Muddiman concludes, "it appears that insulting another politician may be considered a worse offense than stalling or undermining political legislative processes, even though both can have serious consequences."[44] Either way, we tend to be more forgiving when it's an elected official from our own party engaging in the incivility (whether it's name-calling or obstruction) than when the perceived incivility is coming from the opposing party. Third, methods for encouraging productive discourse are being tested and proving effective—even across party lines. Recent experimental research by political scientists Matthew Levendusky and Dominik Stecula finds that cross-party political discussion among ordinary Democrats and Republicans lessens partisan animosity and that these good feelings seem to persist.[45]

If effective self-governance requires us to explore and engage with contrasting ideas and the people who hold these ideas, it is less than encouraging that our collective view of what productive political discussion looks like is a bit blurry. Equally discouraging is the role partisanship plays in our willingness to engage with others and our perceptions of political discourse. Hand-wringing over the state of political discourse today, though, shouldn't obscure the demonstrated value of talking about politics with each other—especially those with whom we disagree. As indicated above, research has demonstrated the democratic value of engaging in difficult discussions—both inside and outside the classroom. How might we put this research into practice?

Talking Like a Democratic Citizen

We're not born knowing how to be a democratic citizen—it's not genetic to understand the integral role of freedom of the press in a system of self-government, or to know how to register to vote, or to have the skill and wherewithal to speak at a public comments portion of a city council meeting. The same holds true for engaging in productive political discussion. The value of holding vibrant and even difficult conversations with others needs to be instilled and the skills to do so need to be fostered. Given the tenor of political conversation today and confusion over its purposes and necessity in democracy, these lessons benefit everyone—from schoolchildren, to college students, to lifelong learners. Indeed, there seems to be a movement building among educators, scholars, and the public at large to proactively address our collective uneasiness about engaging in political discussions, and as a result, a widely accessible toolkit is emerging to help us have these difficult discussions. In the final section of this chapter, I share initiatives and best practices that are being pursued in communities and that have emerged from classrooms that might equip us to engage in this essential element of democracy. If we're going to "keep the republic," we have to be able to talk to each other, but we need the tools to do so.

Lessons from the Classroom

Numerous scholars of civic education have demonstrated the critical importance of integrating the discussion of contemporary political issues and controversies into civic education throughout K–12 education. The combined scholarship indicates that discussing controversial issues in the classroom enhances civic learning and produces positive benefits on students' civic skills, knowledge, and dispositions.[46] This research also offers an important context for us as we embark upon difficult conversations. Beth Rubin's work, for example, offers a perspective that the lived experiences of students with civic life, their civic identities, not only need to be acknowledged by educators but can and should be the foundation for teaching democratic citizenship.[47] This finding extends beyond the relationship between student and teacher—it also applies to interactions between community members. Rooting our conversations in an understanding that our lived experiences with democracy might differ from others' and might affect our relative perceptions of democracy offers a promising route for approaching political discussions.

More and more, higher education is understanding and embracing its role to provide students civic learning opportunities and instill in them the skills and inclination to be engaged citizens. Civic engagement and deliberative democracy pedagogies are teaching approaches taking root on college campuses that recognize the dynamism and action needed in democratic citizens. Building upon the John Dewey adage that "we learn by doing," civic engagement pedagogy holds that college "should include programs that teach such citizenship skills as free deliberation, openness to alternative viewpoints, and critical thinking and should allow a wide variety of ideas to emerge from a diverse group of people."[48] Deliberative pedagogy is grounded in a commitment to connecting the educational experience with the democratic experience and teaching students the skills and mindset of democracy by actively involving them in their learning experience and the college community through opportunities to deliberate, collaborate, and participate.[49] Generally, political discussion can be a valuable way to learn content material while also building the skills associated with political discussion—even when this discussion takes place online.[50]

Again, the lessons learned in the college classroom can be lifelong and broadly applicable. At the Eagleton Institute of Politics on the campus of Rutgers University, my colleague Randi Chmielewski and I created a course focused exclusively on teaching political discussion. Like many campuses, our campus has grappled with issues related to speech and political discourse. Our ongoing seminar for incoming students, "Talking Politics: Disagreeing without Being Disagreeable," is meant to foster an appreciation for such discussion and an enhanced level of comfort with having dialogues that are challenging but productive.[51] Much like this chapter, the underlying premise of the course is that, for democracy to work, citizens need to be able to talk to each other.

The skills taught in the course offer a roadmap, then, for "talking politics" applicable not just to college students but democratic citizens broadly. Specifically, our focus on three core skills—*active listening*, *perspective-taking*, and *fact-checking* (ourselves and others)—offers a foundation for political conversation. With active listening, we're more likely to "disagree without being disagreeable" with others if we feel we've at least been heard. In our classroom, students participate in the "Listening in a Different Way" exercise, in which pairs of students actively listen (without interruption) to their partner's response to a prompt and then respond with a summary and follow-up questions.[52] This one-on-one exercise is challenging but also is a meaningful way not only to alert us to how little we really listen to each other, but also to underscore the importance of building a sense of connection between others as we engage in discussion. Infusing our conversations with perspective-taking encourages a sense of inquiry or an ability to see an issue from someone else's point of view and to be empathetic. As discussed earlier in the chapter, cognitive engagement or gathering information can be both a precursor and an offshoot of other types of political participation. It's essential, though, that we have reliable tools to gather such information. Encouraging fact-checking of ourselves and others lays the groundwork for productive conversations or at least highlights the ways inaccurate information can derail political discussions, challenging us to go into conversations committed to base our assertions on facts and truth.

Community-Level Efforts

Interest, even a sense of urgency, in improving political discourse is developing beyond academia, with efforts taking hold at the community level to bring people together to have difficult but important conversations. A selection is listed below along with a portion of their mission statements—most have both virtual and in-person opportunities to connect.

The Better Arguments Project—"The Better Arguments Project is a national civic initiative created to help bridge divides—not by papering over those divides but by helping people have Better Arguments. In this sense, arguments don't have to drive us apart. Better Arguments can bring us together."[53]

Engaging Differences, a Program at the National Institute for Civic Discourse—"Engaging in conversations across the divide opens doors to finding common ground and moves our country toward a more perfect union. Our programs convey several key principles and best practices that are critical to connecting across divides, including: Empathy instead of vitriol; Listening for Understanding instead of hearing to overpower; and Humility instead of all-knowing. Reflect on those that speak to you, or recall a compelling personal experience."[54]

Living Room Conversations—"We connect people across divides—politics, age, gender, race, nationality, and more—through guided conversations proven to build understanding and transform communities."[55]

The Village Square—"The Village Square is a non-partisan public educational forum on matters of local, state and national importance. We are dedicated to maintaining factual accuracy in civic and political debate by growing civil discourse on divisive issues, and recalling the history and principles at the foundation of our democracy."[56]

In classrooms, on college campuses, in community gathering places, and now even in Zoom rooms, a collective response is taking place to address a shared distaste for the nature of discourse in American politics. Crafting ground rules for political discussion or manufacturing respectful discourse via discussion guides may not be the sort of civic bustle that Tocqueville identified as innate in American democracy and may not reflect the democratic ethos Whitman envisioned, but it should be considered a meaningful start. The growing body of research and practice offer us tools for teaching others and, indeed, teaching ourselves how to have the sort of conversations that self-government requires and build the sort of relationships necessary to fuel a representative democracy.

Much like our aspirational version of American democracy, our vision of the once cordial nature of politics and political discourse might lean closer to myth than reality. That doesn't mean, though, that we can't aspire to interact that way—to aim toward the sort of discourse that befits a healthy and vibrant democracy. And what might that look like? Polite and mannerly is desirable and certainly eases political conversations, but a democracy rooted in freedom, equality, and pluralism also can handle discourse that is loud and even heated—discourse that hears others but that holds them accountable when their views contradict core democratic virtues. Even more important than manners, though, is a willingness to have those conversations and to see such authentic engagement as important and even essential for American democracy. Polite would be nice, but a real commitment to endeavor together and *talk to each other* as democratic citizens is what matters most.

CHAPTER 4

Voting Like a
Democratic Citizen

"The right of citizens of the United States to vote shall not be denied or abridged by the United States or by any State on account of race, color, or previous condition of servitude."
—*Amendment XV, ratified on February 3, 1870*

"The right of citizens of the United States to vote shall not be denied or abridged by the United States or by any State on account of sex."
—*Amendment XIX, ratified on August 18, 1920*

"The right of citizens of the United States, who are eighteen years of age or older, to vote shall not be denied or abridged by the United States or by any State on account of age."
—*Amendment XXVI, ratified on July 1, 1971*

"To make it hard, to make it difficult almost impossible for people to cast a vote is not in keeping with the democratic process."   —*Congressman John Lewis, 2012*

The power to determine who represents us at the local, state, and federal levels of government is the hallmark of a republic,

and fair and equal access to voting is its defining feature. As
the quotes above show, attaining this access has been slow to
become a reality throughout American history, and the struggle continues to this day. Similarly, although Americans profess to place a high value on voting,[1] voting behavior in the
United States also falls short of the ideal—voting rates in
the United States consistently are lower than comparable
democracies, with glaring gaps across elections and groups of
citizens. The mismatch between ideal and reality has much
to do with the way elections are conducted in the United
States—made worse by the intense partisanship marking
contemporary politics.

Although there are legitimate concerns about how the
structure of the electoral process (such as the Electoral College) affects the ability of the majority to translate the vote into
real power, voting still remains a critical tool in holding representatives accountable. Casting a ballot, though, is only one
way "the people" can play a role in determining the makeup
of government—volunteering on a campaign, making campaign contributions, and mobilizing voters are all under-
utilized routes for affecting the outcomes of elections, and
these are routes available to residents no matter their age or
eligibility to vote.

This chapter explores the ways in which residents of all ages
and backgrounds play a role in determining who is elected to
office and the context in which that role is played. Indeed,
being an "informed voter" is more than attaining information
about the candidates running and issues on the ballot—it's
also about understanding the nation's voting process and

its implications for a healthy democracy. Contemporary discussions about voting and electoral law commonly devolve into partisan debates between those claiming voter fraud and those alarmed over voter suppression—rhetoric that has been matched with actions that threaten the legitimacy of electoral processes and outcomes.

In this chapter, I apply the scholarship on voting to the realities of voting in the United States, highlighting the influence institutional factors have on who votes and who doesn't. While applying the theory to the practice of voting might temper the debate, it is not meant to diminish the real threats facing the nation's electoral system currently. Not only are structural changes taking place at the state and local levels that undermine the impartial administration of elections, Americans' confidence in the electoral process has been shaken. An appreciation of the scholarship related to voting not only helps to make sense of the nation's voting; it also serves to inform future action. As such, the chapter concludes with steps to be taken by "the people" in order to "vote like a democratic citizen."

Voting in the United States

The 2020 presidential election was an election like no other. With the nation gripped by the COVID-19 public health crisis, states adjusted election practices to allow citizens to cast their vote without risking their health—with states taking such measures as mailing all residents a ballot to placing secure drop-box locations throughout communities for voters to deposit ballots to avoid crowds on Election Day. The election was notable in another way—voter turnout among Americans hit a record high. With 66.8 percent of citizens eighteen years and older voting, 2020 marked the highest voter turnout of the twenty-first century.[2] According to the Pew Research Center, turnout rates increased in every state compared with 2016, and of the ten states where it rose the most, seven conducted November's vote entirely or mostly by mail.[3] This, of course, raises the question: If 2020 marked record high turnout rates, what were rates like in previous elections and who typically votes in the United States?

Before jumping into an exploration of voter turnout, in the United States alone or in comparison to other democracies, it is important to carefully define the tools of measurement. There are two common ways to quantify voting. Some measures divide the number of people who voted in an election by the number composing the *voting eligible population* (known as VEP) to determine voter turnout. Other measures divide the number of people who voted by the number of *voting age population* (known as VAP) to arrive at a voter turnout rate. Different measures are utilized within the United States and internationally. A voting measure that relies on the voting eligible population is a better measure in that it captures not only those old enough to vote but those also who have the citizenship status to vote or are not precluded from voting due to felony convictions. Often, though, those rates are not easy to access, and researchers will need to either construct the voting eligible population themselves in their analysis or rely on the voting age population as the comparison group.[4]

Who's Voting?

The United States Elections Project, administered by Professor Michael McDonald, has compiled national general election turnout rates of the voting eligible population throughout American history. As McDonald notes, although rates dating from the nation's founding are based on estimates and are certain to contain inaccuracies, they are regarded as the most accurate data available. As shown in figure 5, throughout the 1800s when the franchise was quite limited (mostly to white, male property owners), turnout rates for presidential elections ranged between 70 and 80 percent and between 60 and 70 percent for midterm elections. As the pool of eligible voters increased in size throughout the twentieth century, rates declined, with turnout rates for presidential elections ranging between 50 and 60 percent, and between 40 and 50 percent for midterm elections.

Of those who are turning out on Election Day, to what extent do they represent the populace at large, or are there demographic differences among American voters? Historical trends have demonstrated that there are indeed gaps between those who regularly vote and those who don't, and that levels of income and education, race, and age tend to divide voters and nonvoters. One clear line of demarcation between voters and nonvoters is level of education—the more education a person has, the more likely they are to vote. Data from elections over the last nearly forty years show that citizens with at least some college education vote at rates around 30 percent higher than those without a high

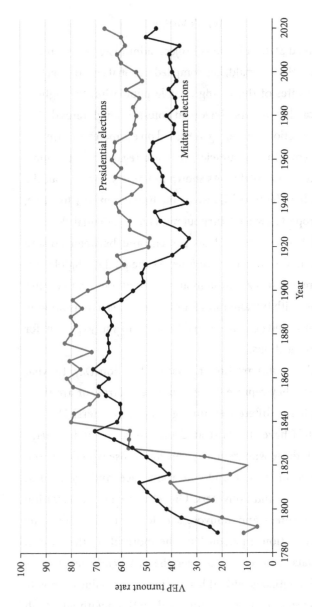

Figure 5. United States VEP Turnout Rates (in percentages), 1789–2022. United States Election Project, Michael P. McDonald, University of Florida, Department of Political Science. http://www.electproject.org /national-1789-present.

school diploma and 10–15 percent higher than those who have completed high school.[5]

Like education, level of income is another strong predictor of voter turnout. In 2020, for example, voter turnout increased as income increased, with the exception of those in the lowest income ranges—the turnout rates of those in income ranges $10,000–$14,999 and $15,000–$19,999 were similar (41–42%). Those with incomes between $100,000 and $149,999 had voter turnout rates of 81.0 percent, while for people whose income was $30,000–$39,999, turnout was 63.6 percent.[6]

There are also consistent gaps in voting along racial and ethnic lines. Although their share of the electorate has decreased over the years, non-Hispanic whites have dominated the electorate when it comes to turnout. With the exception of the elections of 2008 and 2012, when the voting age population of Black voters voted at the highest rates, white voters consistently have the highest rates of turnout.[7]

Another consistent demographic determinant of voting has been age, with young adults voting at much lower rates in midterms and presidential elections than older Americans. For much of the last twenty or so years, rates of turnout for eighteen- to twenty-nine-year-olds for midterm elections have hovered around 20 percent, compared to older Americans' rates in the ranges of 50–60 percent. Prior to 2000, voter turnout rates for young adults were between 30 and 40 percent for presidential contests, but these rates have increased between 2000 and 2016, hovering around 50 percent. Youth voter turnout rates increased again in the 2018 and 2020 elections—with rates jumping from under 20 percent in the 2014 midterms to over 30 percent in 2018, and rates increasing from just over 40 percent to just over 50 percent in 2020.[8]

How Many Are Voting?

Although it marked historic increases in voter turnout in the United States, when it comes to comparable democracies, voter turnout in the United States in 2020 and years prior has been unremarkable. Given the accessibility of comparable data, international comparisons of voting rates often rely on voting estimates based on the voting age population. Such analysis by the Pew Research Center concluded that voting rates of the voting age population in the United States fell short of rates in democracies around the globe in the most recent elections. Comparing America's recent voting rates to measures of voting among a pool of developed democracies, the United States ranked thirty-second. The United States' 2016 turnout rate of 55.7 percent of the voting age population fell behind such countries as Turkey's 2018 rate of 88.9 percent of the VAP, Australia's rate of 80.7 percent in 2019, France's rate of 67.9 percent in 2017, and the United Kingdom's 2019 voting rate of 62.3 percent.[9]

A few explanations are in order, though. Australia and other democracies around the globe such as Belgium and Luxembourg have a form of compulsory voting in place—one in which a fine or penalty is imposed for not voting.[10] Clearly, this elevates rates of turnout. Other nations, such as Turkey, may have high rates of turnout but have not exhibited support for the values intrinsic in "liberal democracies," as discussed in chapter 2—voting rates may be high, but such democratic tenets as freedom of speech and the press or fair and impartial juries have been undermined by those in power. Still, the United States has not led the democratic world when it comes to voting. In many ways, this lag reflects the manner in which the country holds elections. America's electoral system also helps to explain why some get to the polls consistently and others do not.

THE PATCHWORK OF AMERICA'S ELECTORAL SYSTEM AND ITS EFFECTS ON TURNOUT

One of the groups of voters who turned out in large numbers in 2020 was young adults. Among eligible eighteen- to twenty-nine-year-olds, up to 50 percent voted in the election between Joe Biden and Donald Trump—an increase of 11 percent from 2016.[11] In New Jersey, voting rates among young adults stood at a whopping 67 percent—the highest youth vote in the country. Other states saw notable increases in youth turnout and reported strong voting rates—Maine's youth voter turnout stood at 61 percent (an increase of 6% from 2016), Connecticut's rate of 54 percent was an 11 percent increase from 2016, and Vermont reported a youth voting rate of 49 percent (an increase of 12% from the previous election).[12]

What accounts for these increases? To be sure, voting among young adults is a function of many factors including political socialization by parents and civic education in schools. In 2020, the closeness of the election and the polarizing nature of the Donald Trump candidacy surely galvanized young adults to turn out on Election Day. Analysis by the Center for Information and Research on Civic Learning and

Engagement (CIRCLE), though, reveals a notable similarity among states with strong youth voting rates and stark increases from the previous contest—the way in which the election was conducted in that state.

Election Practices and Differences at the State Level

In New Jersey, for example, registered young adults were automatically sent a ballot whether or not they requested it, were automatically registered to vote thanks to a state law passed in 2018,[13] and are able to "preregister" to vote in advance of their eighteenth birthday.[14] As a result, voting among New Jersey's youngest eligible voters increased a remarkable 22 percent from the previous election. CIRCLE's analysis indicates that youth voting rates were highest and had the largest increases in turnout in those states in which eligible young voters were automatically sent a ballot. Similarly, states that had other measures that facilitated youth voting such as online voter registration or same-day voter registration had higher youth voting rates on average than those that did not.[15] Accounting for the voting rates of Americans compared to other democratic citizens around the globe or the comparable voting rates between Americans requires an accounting of how the United States conducts elections.

There are a few key features that distinguish the United States' electoral system that set it apart from other democracies. For much of the nation's history and for a good number of voters, the country's electoral system has been set up in such a way that the responsibility for getting oneself registered to vote and to the polls falls predominantly on the voter. It has only been in recent years and only in a selection of states, for example, that voters were automatically registered to vote—for most, it is the responsibility of the individual to get themselves registered to vote. This one quality of America's electoral system has had a profound impact on who votes and who doesn't in the United States, and political science scholarship has long pointed to America's voter registration laws as a key factor in explaining the country's comparably lower voter turnout rates.[16]

The other distinguishing feature is the great variety among states in how they conduct elections. Indeed, much of the responsibility of determining how elections will be conducted—registration practices, residency requirements, methods of voting—lies with individual states and results in a patchwork of election practices. These factors can uniquely burden some citizens over others and affect who shows up at the polls.

Voting and the Constitution

Interestingly, the U.S. Constitution has little to say about voting—most references to voting can be found in the amendments to the Constitution. More remarkably, the Constitution confers no affirmative "right" to vote. As Kim Wehle writes in her book *What You Need to Know about Voting and Why*, "the US Constitution does not contain language explicitly preserving the right to vote. It doesn't state, for example, that 'the right to vote shall not be circumscribed,' or anything of the sort. This may come as a surprise, because voting is the foundation for American democracy."[17] Rather than affirmatively granting the right to vote in the Constitution itself, it is through the amendments that the government is barred from discriminating against categories of citizens seeking access to the ballot—the Fourteenth and Fifteenth Amendments enfranchised African American men, the Nineteenth Amendment afforded women access to the vote, the Twenty-Third Amendment allowed residents of the District of Columbia to elect delegates to the Electoral College, and the Twenty-Sixth Amendment granted access to the ballot for eighteen-year-olds.[18] Of the few references to voting in the Constitution itself, the mention in Article 1, Section 4 has had a profound impact on voting history in the United States. It is in this portion of the Constitution that individual states are empowered to determine their election practices.

As a result, the nation's electoral system consists of an assortment of voter registration and Election Day practices—some of which enhance and enable voting and others that dampen it.[19] For example, as of 2021, a total of twenty states and Washington, D.C., had in place some version of same-day registration allowing qualified residents of the state to register to vote and cast a ballot at the same time. Of those states, eighteen and Washington, D.C., allow voters to both register and vote on Election Day.[20] Deadlines for registration vary in the remaining states—some stipulating that one must be registered twenty-eight to thirty days before an election, some setting the deadline twenty to twenty-seven days before an election, and one state (North Dakota) has no voter registration system.[21] For most states now, voter registration is not only offered or conducted by paper forms but also online.[22] Although the age requirement for voting in state and federal elections is eighteen, some states allow young potential voters to preregister to vote (some as early as age sixteen) so they are ready to vote when they reach voting age.[23]

The Effects of Election Practices on Voting

Research on the effects of these varying registration systems on voting behavior consistently demonstrates that those states with more accessible and less burdensome voter registration requirements have higher voter turnout rates or, in sum, that voter registration practices can depress turnout.[24] Although the causal relationship between voter registration and turnout is widely agreed upon, the magnitude of the effect varies based on research design and context. Studies that compare rates between states with different registration requirements either by using aggregate turnout data[25] or by using survey data to estimate the effects of more liberal registration requirements conclude that more facilitative voter registration laws can increase turnout by up to 10 percent.[26] Scholars who have focused their research on differences in registration practices within a state conclude that although there is a positive relationship between easier voter registration and higher turnout rates, such laws may not boost turnout as significantly as commonly understood.[27] The date of registration closing specifically, though, has been shown to make a significant impact, with earlier deadlines effectively closing out portions of the electorate (recently moved in particular) and thereby dampening turnout.[28]

Likewise, voting practices across the country also vary widely, with each state constructing its own set of regulations and procedures regarding such matters as early voting, voting by mail, polling locations, drop-off locations for ballots, and required voter identification. Even the nomenclature varies widely—for example, early in-person voting has been referred to as "early voting," "in-person absentee voting," and "advanced voting."[29] The details and differences between states' electoral systems are too numerous and too much in flux to recount here. Much like voter registration, though, there is a growing body of research on the effects of voting practices on voter turnout—a body of research that continues to grow as states explore and adopt new systems including all-mail elections and early in-person voting.

As Burden and colleagues indicate in their review, this research shows fairly consistently that states with election day registration (EDR), allowing voters who have not registered to vote to register and cast their ballot on Election Day, have higher voter turnout rates, with EDR boosting turnout up to 7 percent.[30] Teasing out the relationship between the other voting methods and voter turnout is not as clear-cut. Gronke, Galanes-Rosenbaum, and Miller found in their 2007 research that only early voting by mail, a system in which all voters receive and cast their ballots via regular mail, has a clearly positive impact on voter turnout, but that early in-person voting has only negligible positive results. In fact, Burden and colleagues build upon this finding and assert that early in-person voting used alone actually can decrease voter turnout—in part, because it dampens voter mobilization activities by parties and campaigns, which is a critical determinant of voting.[31] Indeed, research on the effects of a state's voting infrastructure suggests that there is no one surefire method to produce high voter turnout—other explanatory variables such as mobilization, the quality of one's political socialization from parents, and a potential voter's level of education and income work in relationship with other factors and may explain the effectiveness (or lack thereof) of voting reforms.[32]

GAPS IN THE VOTING SYSTEM

This conclusion underscores the necessity of recognizing and addressing the inequities inherent in the manner in which the United States conducts elections. In a system in which practices vary widely between states and registering is primarily the voter's responsibility, the burdens associated with casting one's ballot do not fall evenly. As highlighted earlier, the pool of active and consistent voters historically has been divided according to levels of education and income as well as age. Even the only somewhat unifying feature of the nation's electoral system—Election Day—is enjoyed unevenly. Established not by the Constitution, but by legislation passed by the 28th Congress in 1845, elections for federal offices are to be held on the Tuesday after the first Monday in November in even-numbered years.[33] The timing of Election Day is another feature, then, that must be factored into one's calculus when planning to vote—potentially impeding the voting behavior of segments of the populace. Although legislation established its date, Election Day isn't a federal holiday. Voters must navigate professional, academic, and personal responsibilities in order to cast their ballot, which can be difficult for those who have less flexibility in those areas of their lives.

Voting in the United States takes resources—time, education, skill, stability. The unequal burden of the nation's voting infrastructure has been a long-standing conclusion in political science, and it is a conclusion that has held steady. Verba and Nie's 1972 classic *Participation in America* demonstrated the causal link between socioeconomic status and voting behavior (as well as other types of civic behavior), with Wolfinger and Rosenstone's subsequent study *Who Votes* (1980) attributing education and age as the most significant demographic determinants of voting. Building upon those conclusions, Rosenstone and Hansen's 1993 study highlighted the impact of the strategic mobilization of voters by parties and campaigns that often amplifies demographic divisions in the pool of likely and unlikely voters.

Indeed, it often is not enough to want to vote or to "think like a democratic citizen"; it is the context in which possible voters must operate that affects "voting like a democratic citizen." All of this is not to say that voting reforms such as in-person early voting shouldn't be attempted or aren't effective. Instead, it is important to look at the voting system as a whole and not just reforms in isolation. For example, it is not enough to institute a vote-by-mail system—such a reform must also include a vigorous public education plan that reaches out specifically to those vulnerable populations who might not appreciate the changes to voting practices. Similarly, it is not enough to encourage reforms to voter registration practices—young adults' political interest and sense of public responsibility must be sparked with a vibrant civic education system.

Low voter turnout rates in the United States in relation to other similar democracies, then, have a good deal to do with the way elections are conducted. Differences in voting rates within the United States also can be explained in large part by the nation's electoral infrastructure—who it serves and who it doesn't. To what extent, though, is the way the United States holds elections an extension of the way the nation thinks about voting and about democracy itself? How have our conceptions of individuality, equality, unity, popular sovereignty, and the rule of law been reflected in the way we hold elections, and even contemporary perceptions and practices related to the legitimacy of elections? Our common perception of whether or not voting is a right or a privilege offers a window.

LINKING AMERICANS' THOUGHTS ABOUT VOTING TO THE PRACTICE OF VOTING

The United States is often referred to as the world's longest functioning democracy. Some argue, though, that the nation only became a true democracy in the 1960s with the passage of the Voting Rights Act, when African Americans were fully enfranchised—nearly 200 years after the Declaration of Independence.[34] As stated at the outset, full and equal access to the polls has been an evolving process throughout the nation's history—one secured by a succession of amendments to the U.S. Constitution and the passage of various pieces legislation by the U.S. Congress. And yet still, voting is up for debate.

At the time of this writing, there is a struggle regarding passage of the "For the People Act" (H.R. 1), which passed the House in March of 2021 and its Senate counterpart, the "Freedom to Vote Act"—legislative packages that seek to reform voting, redistricting, and campaign finance.[35] Compounding this struggle are actions taken in the wake of the 2020 election and in advance of subsequent elections that fundamentally alter the state-level practice of elections and threaten confidence in the outcomes of future elections. These struggles highlight divisions between political parties and portions of the population on conceptualizations of voting and its regulation.

Again, the body of the Constitution does not assertively grant a right to vote—it us in the amendments that such language is provided. Even without those explicit statements of a "right to vote" (for women, African Americans, etc.), as Kimberly Wehle argues, voting is elemental to a representative democracy: "voting is important not because the right to vote appears in the Constitution (it doesn't), but because voting preserves all other constitutional rights. It's the linchpin for everything else."[36]

Perceptions of Voting

Recent survey research highlights that perceptions of voting—as either a "right" or a "privilege"—fall along partisan lines and demographic background. In a survey conducted by the Pew Research Center, a majority (57%) asserted that voting is "a fundamental right for every adult U.S. citizen and should not be restricted in any way," and 42 percent held that "voting is a privilege that comes with responsibilities and can be limited if adult U.S. citizens don't meet some requirements." In large numbers (78%), Democratic and Democratic-leaning respondents hold that voting is a fundamental right that should not be restricted in any way. In contrast, 67 percent of Republican and Republican-learning respondents believe that voting is a privilege that can be limited if requirements are not met.

This same survey research also showed that perceptions of voting as a right or privilege also break down along ethnic and racial lines, age, and education—the same sorts of demographic fault lines in the voter turnout data referenced earlier in the chapter. African American respondents were the most likely racial and ethnic group to view voting as a fundamental right—white respondents were the least likely. Also, younger adults (forty-nine years or younger) were more likely than older adults to conceive of voting as a right, and those with more education also viewed voting less as a privilege than a right.[37]

Legislating (and Adjudicating) Voting Today

The partisan differences about voting are reflected in national debates and legislative actions taken in recent years on the topic of voting. In addition to the constitutional amendments outlined earlier, there has been a series of legislative actions over the last fifty years that have shaped voting in the United States—the Voting Rights Act of 1965 that tackled barriers to voting erected during the era of Jim Crow, the expansion of the Voting Rights Act in 1975 to protect language minorities groups, the Motor Voter Law in 1993 that required states to offer opportunities to register to vote when acquiring or renewing a driver's license, 1990's Americans with Disabilities Act that prohibits banning people from voting due to disability, and the Help America Vote Act (2002) that mandates voting upgrades and created the Election Assistance Commission.[38]

In 1965, support for voting rights legislation was less a reflection of one's political party, and more a reflection of the region of the country a member of Congress represented. In the Senate, the Voting Rights Act passed by a 77–19 vote on May 26, 1965 (the party breakdown of the Senate was 68 Democrats and 32 Republicans at the time). Notably, senators voting in favor of the bill included several Republicans such as Senator George Aiken from Vermont, Senator Bourke Hickenlooper from Iowa, and Senator Milton Young from North Dakota. In contrast, a number of Democratic senators representing southern states voted in opposition—Senator Harry Byrd from Virginia, Senator Allen Ellender from Louisiana, and Senator Sam Ervin from North Carolina.[39] The House of Representatives (then composed of 295 Democrats and 140 Republicans) debated the bill for over a month but then passed the Voting Rights Act on July 9, 1965, by a vote of 333–85.[40]

Over fifty years later, the subject of voting and public policy regulating voting figures prominently in the national debate, serving as a stark example of the nation's current political divisions. Much of this current debate is rooted in the 2013 Supreme Court decision in *Shelby County vs. Holder*, in which the court ruled that portions of the Voting Rights Act requiring certain states to obtain a preclearance prior to making changes to voting practices do not reflect current conditions in the affected states and therefore is an unconstitutional burden and violation of states' power to regulate elections. The case was decided by a vote of five to four, and Chief Justice John Roberts explained the decision to invalidate the formula crafted in 1965 necessary for preclearance, writing, "At the time, the coverage formula—the means of linking the exercise of the unprecedented authority with the problem that warranted it—made sense. . . . Nearly 50 years later, things have changed dramatically. Shelby County contends that the preclearance requirement, even without regard to its disparate coverage, is now unconstitutional. Its arguments have a good deal of force."

In her dissent, Justice Ginsberg asserted that the success of the requirement for preclearance does not justify jettisoning it. "Throwing out preclearance when it has worked and is continuing to work to stop discriminatory changes is like throwing away your umbrella in a rainstorm because you are not getting wet."[41]

The *Shelby* decision ushered in a wave of changes to electoral practices across the country, including in those jurisdictions that previously had been subject to close scrutiny. The Brennan Center for Justice at NYU Law reports that in the aftermath of the decision, states that previously had been required to obtain preclearance began to purge voters from registration rolls at higher rates than those states that had not been covered by the preclearance requirement,[42] and that a number of states began to enact more stringent voting laws than they had in previous elections, including requiring voter identification and altering absentee ballots and early voting processes.[43]

The vigor of the debate and the pace of state-level policy-making related to voting has only intensified in subsequent presidential and midterm elections, and given the volume, cannot all be detailed here. Still, it has been the events surrounding recent elections and reaching a crescendo with the insurrection of January 6, 2021, that have left the United States unsteady and divided as we look ahead to future elections.

- The tightly contested 2016 presidential race between Donald Trump and Hillary Rodham Clinton resulted in Trump winning the necessary Electoral College votes to secure the White House, although he had lost the popular vote.
- Subsequent to the election, evidence emerged of interference by the Russian government, with evidence of contact with the Trump campaign.
- As a counter to the narrative that the outcome of the election was illegitimate, the Trump administration claimed the election had been marked by voter fraud and formed a Presidential Commission on Election Integrity. The Commission disbanded in 2018 without presenting any evidence.[44]
- The 2018 contest brought out an increased interest in voting but also a wave of changes to electoral practices around the country, including the closing of polling locations—particularly in urban areas serving minority voters.[45]
- The historic 2020 presidential election was marked not only by adjustments to voting practices to protect public

health and record high voter turnout, but election outcomes were contested at the state level in ways that had never been seen, with an unprecedented amount of litigation generated in the effort.[46]

- Teams of protestors, insurrectionists, and members of white nationalist militias violently stormed the Capitol to disrupt and halt the certification of the Electoral College declaring Joe Biden president of the United States.[47] Nine deaths have been attributed to the events of that day.[48]

- State-level election audits or ballot reviews by third-party contractors, such as the review ordered by the Arizona State Senate and conducted by the firm Cyber Ninjas, sowed doubt about election outcomes even though the expertise and impartiality of these reviewers have been called into question.[49]

- State legislatures around the country have introduced legislation, and in many instances been successful at altering election practices and oversight, taking responsibility out of the hands of impartial election experts. Alterations that in effect criminalize election administration and place reviews of the elections in the hands of the legislature have been cited as particularly egregious threats to fair and professional elections that reflect the will of the people.[50]

- Federal legislation addressing voting, such as the For the People Act (H.R. 1) and the John R. Lewis Voting Rights Advancement Act (H.R. 4), have stalled in Congress, mired in partisan division. H.R. 4, a response to the *Shelby* decision, establishes new criteria for determining which states must obtain preclearance before making voting changes. It passed the House along party lines— 219 Democrats voted in favor and all 212 Republicans opposed.[51] A more broad package of voting reforms addressing voter access, election integrity and security, campaign finance, and ethics, H.R. 1 also passed the House along party lines (one Democrat joined all of the Republican members of the House in opposing the bill).[52] Neither bill has progressed in the Senate.

This summary brings the conversation back to the question of how Americans think about voting and how that is reflected in the nation's actions. The quickened pace of changes to state and local voting practices is clear, with supporters justifying these actions as an extension of states' rights or fraud protection and opponents asserting that they are tantamount to voter suppression. Given the data and scholarship cited earlier in this chapter, changes in election practices being undertaken at the state level promise to be deleterious to potential voters— especially to those most burdened by the nation's electoral infrastructure.

Confidence in the Voting Process

More troublesome is the partisan-driven lack of confidence that has been sown in electoral administration and outcomes, with:

- An overwhelming majority of Trump voters indicating that the 2020 election was not run well compared to the Biden voters who believe it was run well;[53]

- Partisan divisions regarding enacting practices to enhance access to the ballot, with declines in support among Republicans for such practices as automatic voter registration and no-excuse absentee voting as well as increased support among Republicans for removing inactive voters from voter registration lists;[54]
- An overwhelming percentage of Democratic voters expressing confidence that those ineligible to vote are kept from voting compared to only about 30 percent of Republicans.[55]

Lack of confidence in elections is not entirely new, and there is research to indicate that voter confidence often is shaken when one's candidate has lost.[56] Still, what is less characteristic have been the actions altering the practice and acceptance of elections and the sharp partisan divisions motivating these actions. Again, preparing to vote or being an "informed voter" requires an appreciation not only of the composition of our ballot but an understanding of the construction and administration of the voting system—its strengths and its shortcomings. This chapter concludes, then, with steps to be taken by "the people" in order to "vote like a democratic citizen" and to ensure that others are able to do so also.

Voting Like a Democratic Citizen

The vote is the essential element of a republican form of government. The electoral process, though, is imbued with a set of values and expectations in liberal democracies such as the

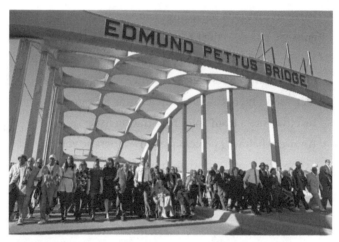

Figure 6. President Barack Obama, First Lady Michelle
Obama, Marian Robinson, Malia Obama, and Sasha Obama
join Rep. John Lewis, former President George W. Bush, former
First Lady Laura Bush, former foot soldiers, and other dignitar-
ies in marching across the Edmund Pettus Bridge to commem-
orate the fiftieth anniversary of Bloody Sunday and the
Selma-to-Montgomery civil rights marches, at the Edmund
Pettus Bridge in Selma, Alabama. Photograph by Pete Souza,
National Archives.

United States—that not only each eligible citizen has the freedom to vote, but that there is a shared commitment to enable
all citizens to vote; that the unique features of states, locali-
ties, and even voters are acknowledged, but that there also is
a shared commitment to cohesion and the good of the republic when administering elections and affirming their outcomes;
that actions taken to empower the people to vote are pursued
within the rule of law. Given the scholarship shared in this
chapter, how does one operationalize these goals? By voting,

by helping others vote, and by participating in other activities that support the electoral process and that help to determine who represents us in public office.

Make a Plan to Vote and Vote

In addition to the oftentimes confusing nature of America's electoral system, the sheer number of elections the nation and its states hold can make active citizenship a challenge. Residents of New Jersey, for example, vote in federal elections for president and the U.S. Congress in even-numbered years but also hold elections for governor and the state legislature in odd-numbered years—each consisting of both primary and general elections.[57] Although the bar may be high, voting consistently in every election is one important way to put the ideals of democratic citizenship into action. As this chapter has demonstrated, it often is the actions taken by state legislatures or city councils that have the most profound impact on our daily lives and the contours of democracy. And yet it is those elections that tend to have the lowest voter turnout. Using New Jersey as an example again, voter turnout rates for the 2021 election in which voters were electing both a governor and the entire state legislature were 40 percent, with turnout in some counties standing at just 30 percent.[58] In a state-level election of consequence, then, 60 percent of those who will be governed by the elected governor and state legislature did not play a part in determining who these public officials will be. True representation requires voting rates that represent the public. As women's rights and suffragist activist Susan B. Anthony stated, "Someone struggled for your right to vote. Use it."[59]

Help Others Vote

Another way to fuse the principles of democracy and the research shared in this chapter is by helping others vote—not only by facilitating their voting experience but by advancing equal access to the polls. Unique in a variety of ways, the manner in which the United States conducts elections can be particularly burdensome for those with limited time, education, and economic stability. Supporting individuals as they seek accurate information about voter registration deadlines, polling locations, and vote-by-mail regulations is an extension of the democratic commitment to voting. Thankfully, there are a number of nonpartisan efforts at the state and national levels designed strictly for that purpose—sharing reliable, nonpartisan, and state-specific information on how to get registered and cast one's vote.[60] As President Kennedy stated, "The rights of every man are diminished when the rights of one man are threatened." In that spirit, looking to research rather than rhetoric and supporting policies and practices that ensure equal access to the polls is also an extension of one's commitment to democratic governance. The 2020 election demonstrated that practices such as vote-by-mail offer a method of voting that draws voters and that nonpartisan election audits have shown to be secure and reliable. From recognizing the disparate impact of such decisions as limiting drop box locations for ballots to acknowledging that some reforms can be burdensome and spark resistance among election officials,[61] challenging ourselves to be driven by data *and* democratic principles when it comes to electoral policies reflects democratic rather than partisan loyalty.

Support Candidates and Campaigns

Finally, although fundamental, voting is just one way residents can determine who represents them in local, state, and federal bodies of government. There are numerous other ways, both nonpartisan and party- or campaign-related, that eligible and non-eligible voters alike can pursue to determine who represents us in public office. Participating in nonpartisan voter registration or get-out-the-vote drives is an activity beyond voting that raises awareness and helps to reduce the costs associated with voting (such as determining voter registration deadlines or polling locations) and heightens potential voters' likelihood of casting a ballot. There are numerous other campaign-related activities, though, that offer opportunities to support the election of a particular candidate—canvassing or phone-banking for a candidate, distributing campaign signs or buttons, making campaign contributions. These are activities in which all can participate no matter their age or voting eligibility, and upon which candidates rely, but often are overlooked as methods of political participation. For example, a 2021 survey of young adults conducted biannually by Harvard's Institute of Politics found that large majorities do not tend to pursue these campaign activities: 86 percent indicated that they hadn't participated in a government, political, or issue-related organization in the previous twelve months; 69 percent hadn't shared or posted online advocating for a political position or opinion; 80 percent hadn't donated money to a political campaign or cause; and 88 percent had not volunteered on a political campaign for a candidate or an issue.[62]

Conclusion

Equal access to the ballot has not come easily or quickly in the United States. Although the passage of the Fifteenth Amendment in 1870 eliminated race as a barrier to voting, it wasn't until the passage of the Voting Rights Act in 1965 that the benefits of that amendment were truly put into practice—benefits that currently are under threat. Although eighteen-year-olds were granted access to the ballot in 1970, voter turnout gaps by age persist, with partisan divisions on implementing voting practices that successfully bridge those gaps. Despite the development of successful models of electoral practices, both here and abroad, the nation consists of an ever-changing patchwork of voter registration and Election Day practices that benefit some and burden others. Nearly 250 years since the writing of the Declaration of Independence, large portions of the populace regard voting as a privilege and not a fundamental right. In short, voting in the United States' democratic republic continues to be the subject of contention.

It is worth remembering, though, that democratic advances throughout American history have been driven by sustained, broad, popular commitment and activism—civil rights activists, women's rights activists, social and political movements. Indeed, what is required today is a shared willingness by "the people" to put the complicated ideals of American democracy into practice at the ballot box—not just for themselves but for their fellow democratic citizens. Indeed, as Congressman John Lewis suggests, the antidote to measures that undermine the vitality of democracy's election process is action. "Sometimes you have to not just dream about what could be—you get out and push, and you pull, and you preach. And you create a climate and environment to get those in high places, to get men and women of goodwill in power to act."[63]

CHAPTER 5

Acting Like a
Democratic Citizen

"The job of being an alert active citizen is exciting, relatively easy, and wholly rewarding. My many years of civic work—as a citizen and as a public official—convinced me that if each one of us did his or her share and lived up to the spirit of this oath, that his town, his nation, and the world would be a happier and a very better place to live in. In this I believe."
—*Genevieve B. Earle, 1885–1956*

Begun in the 1950s by journalist Edward R. Murrow, *This I Believe* was a radio program consisting of a series of essays composed by both prominent and everyday citizens capturing their core values and the beliefs shaping their lives. In its early years, listeners could hear essays by such prominent figures as Eleanor Roosevelt and Jackie Robinson as well as by civic and corporate leaders and writers and artists. In later years, the project was taken up by National Public Radio and since has been incorporated and serves as an online resource for educators and the public at large.[1] One of those who composed a *This I Believe* essay was Genevieve B. Earle.

Though not well known, Earle seems to have been the model citizen. From Brooklyn and a graduate of Adelphi University,

Earle's work as a social worker led to a life of service that included founding the Women's City Club in 1917, serving on the City Board of Child Welfare, and serving as president of Brooklyn's League of Women Voters chapter. Even more notable was that Earle was the first woman elected to the New York City Council in 1937 and went on to serve five terms representing Brooklyn.[2] In her *This I Believe* essay entitled "The Job of Citizenship," Earle expressed her belief in the positive power of good government and active citizenship, writing, "Archimedes explained the principle of fulcrum by saying, 'Show me the place to stand and I can move the world.' To me, this place is city government; touch that and you touch the whole community. Thus the weight of a finger at the right place can set in motion forces that can create a wholesome, decent environment for all people and mold our way of living a little nearer to our heart's desire."[3] Though written in a very different era, these words regarding the role of the citizen ring true today.

In a representative democracy, the "job of citizenship" goes well beyond the act of voting. Critically important as it is, electing individuals to represent us in office is just one part of our responsibility—not only must we hold public officials accountable and communicate our wishes to them as they are serving, we ourselves must be willing to play a part in the running of democracy. Playing an active role in the civic life of our communities through volunteering is an essential element of democratic citizenship, as is serving on boards or commissions and even running for office. In short, the "job of citizenship" is full-time and extends well beyond Election Day.

This chapter explores what it means to act like a democratic citizen—to express our political voices to those we've elected to political office, to run for and serve in office, and to play a vibrant role in the life of our communities. As in previous chapters, I'll explore the connection between these behaviors and democracy's health and vitality, chart Americans' propensity to engage in these democratic actions and the factors undergirding these actions, and offer a call that we collectively elevate the importance of these democratic actions in our quest to "keep the republic."

Speaking Out

The day after the inauguration of President Donald Trump, hundreds of thousands of people in Washington, D.C., and millions around the globe came out to protest and take to the streets for the "Women's March." A response to a campaign viewed as misogynistic in tone and hostile to marginalized groups, the purpose was to vocally and visibly speak out.[4] The 2017 Women's March is just one in a series of relatively recent high-profile national protest movements; a few of the more visible efforts include the March for Our Lives movement that formed in response to the shooting at Marjorie Stoneman Douglas High School in Florida[5] and the Black Lives Matter movement that was galvanized after the acquittal of Trayvon Martin's killer and is dedicated to eradicating violence against Black communities.[6]

Of course, these recent and quite visible efforts build on a long tradition of grassroots movements that have taken place

Figure 7. Vietnam draft resistance march at Yale University in New Haven, Connecticut. Photograph by Robert Child, *New Haven Journal Courier*. Courtesy of the National Archives.

throughout the nation's history, from protests demanding women's suffrage to the March on Selma and the bus boycotts of the civil rights movement to the student protests surrounding America's involvement in Vietnam. As David Meyer notes in *The Politics of Protest*, the social movements that produce protests enjoy a "dynamic interaction with the political mainstream" and are in many ways a function of the system of government established by the Framers of the Constitution— one that establishes civil liberties, encourages coalition building, and is composed of elected officials who hope to be reelected.[7]

Protests are just one of many ways in which democratic citizens can express their political views. Using one's "public voice" also can include contacting public officials, contacting the media, petitioning, participating in a boycott, or any other activity in which "citizens give expression to their views on public issues."[8] In his book *The Future of Democracy*, Peter Levine extends the list of methods of expressive engagement to include "displaying a sign, bumper sticker, or button; wearing a T-shirt with a social or political message; using a credit card that gives some of its profit to a social cause; operating or participating in a political blog; contributing time or money to an advocacy group or think tank; and boycotting or 'buycotting.'"[9]

The Democratic Role of Expressing Our Political Voice

What is the purpose of these expressive activities and how do they connect with democratic citizenship? If voting is about determining who represents us in office, speaking out through such means as protesting, contacting your elected officials, or speaking at a public hearing is about influencing the actions of those serving in positions of power. Even more, public expressions of political views also might be aimed at shifting public opinion on an issue or even corporate practices.[10] Indeed, holding those in power accountable—from one's congressperson to a CEO to the citizenry—is intrinsic to the "job of citizenship" and reflects an active and engaged type of democratic citizenship. Even more, the commensurate value of each citizen's political participation is reflective of the vitality of political equality in a democracy. As the authors of *Voice and Equality* state at the outset of their landmark text, "Voice and equality are central to democratic participation. In a meaningful democracy, the people's voice must be clear and loud—clear so that policymakers understand citizen concerns and loud so that they have an incentive to pay attention to what's said. Since democracy implies not only governmental responsiveness to citizen interests but also equal consideration of the interests of each citizen, democratic participation must also be equal."[11]

Rates of Expressive Engagement

So much attention focuses on the explicitly democratic action of voting (with the attendant concerns regarding turnout rates), but we rarely consider the extent to which people engage in democracy by speaking out. How many Americans express their political voices in ways other than casting a ballot? More importantly, perhaps, who participates in these actions and what sort of impact do they make? These questions were central to Verba, Schlozman, and Brady's 1995 classic *Voice and Equality*. Using a large representative sample capturing not only a cross-section of the populace but those really engaged in the many facets of political participation,[12] the authors found at the time of their study that for most Americans, voting is their only form of political action. Specifically, the authors found that 71 percent of their sample were active voters (registered voters who had a history of voting consistently in national and local elections). In contrast, only 34 percent of those studied were active in contacting federal or local government officials or agencies (either in person or on the phone) about public problems or concerns. Even fewer looked to protests as a way of expressing their political voice—Verba, Schlozman, and Brady found that only 6 percent of their sample had participated in a protest, march, or demonstration regarding a national or local issue in the last two years.[13]

Given the visibility of protests in recent years, it is worth considering whether more Americans are extending their political action beyond voting and are expressing their political voice today in other ways than in past years. Data gathered over time by Gallup indicates that more Americans today at least feel driven to participate in a protest than Americans did fifty years ago. In an August 2018 public opinion poll conducted by Gallup, 36 percent of those surveyed indicated that they had felt the urge to protest—an increase from 10 percent in 1965, which many would consider a moment of great political tumult in the United States.[14]

Some twenty-five years after *Voice and Equality*, David Meyer asserts that the use of protest in the United States "remains a critical political tactic for a wide variety of causes."[15] Moreover, he concludes that the use of protest has become a more common political activity and has become more widespread, with broader constituencies utilizing it as a form of political action leading to what he refers to as the "institutionalization of protest as a political tactic . . . an add-on or component of the political strategy of an increasingly broad range of groups."[16] Indeed, the use of protest has "moved from being a sporadic feature of American politics to being one that is perpetual; protest is used with greater frequency, is used by more diverse constituencies, and is used to represent a wider range of claims than ever before."[17]

Accessibility of Expressive Advocacy

The increased use of protest as a form of expressing one's political voice might be viewed as favorable—the nobility of the Freedom Riders, for example, during the civil rights movement might be just the sort of political engagement we would want to emulate today. It is worth considering, though, why protests have become more common, and more importantly, who gains from the rise of protest as a method. If democracy's health is measured by the equality of political participation, Verba, Schlozman, and Brady's research found that those most likely to express their political voice beyond the act of voting represented a narrow slice of the citizenry, unrepresentative of its diversity and needs, but with the capacity and the networks that allow them platforms for expressing their opinions. One of the authors' central conclusions in *Voice and Equality* is that different forms of political participation—from voting to working on a campaign to protesting to contacting a public official—require different sets of resources from the citizens. Some activities require just time and others require not just time but also skills and money.[18] Many may want to engage in political activities beyond voting but don't have the capacity to do so or aren't recruited to participate by nonpolitical institutions such as civic or voluntary associations.[19]

Meyer's research offers a similar caution about the equality of voices represented in activities outside the voting booth. For Meyer, the institutionalization of protests as a political tactic erodes their grassroots nature and their fundamental purpose to provide a megaphone for those without a voice, "protests are coordinated by professional social movement organizations that derive their legitimacy, at least in part, from participation in movements. As protest becomes routine, less disruptive, and more accepted, we have to wonder whether movements become less important, particularly to those who formerly depended upon them."[20] As the authors of *Voice and Equality* posited, it is justifiable to question the accessibility of these expressions of political voice and, consequently, the quality of their representation.

The Impact of Speaking Out

It is also worth exploring the efficacy of expressive advocacy in general, and protests specifically. Do they make a difference? How and for whom? There's plenty of scholarship that has long asserted that the effects of expressive advocacy and the political voice of the masses are limited when it comes to affecting policy. If historically protests have been composed of the marginalized, research by such scholars as Larry Bartels and Martin Gillens has shown that inequality in income translates into inequality in the polices enacted by those in power.[21] Using multivariate analysis, Gillens and Page found in 2014 that economic elites and organized groups representing business interests have substantial independent impacts on U.S. government policy, while average citizens and mass-based interest groups have little or no independent influence.[22]

In "Protest Is Not Enough," a 1984 study of the effectiveness of protest and mobilization on representation and policy in urban settings throughout California, the authors found variety in the openness and responsiveness in local power structures to incorporating the demands and seeing to the needs of Black and Hispanic residents. The authors' "theory of political incorporation" holds that protests might prompt electoral engagement, but that is insufficient to really achieve political equality. "Incorporation, in turn, depends on the determined mobilization of minority resources in the electoral arena. Although demand-protest often contributes to electoral mobilization, demand-protest alone is not enough to produce strong incorporation of minority interests in city government."[23] Protests might serve as a precursor or a spark, but achieving political power requires electing those from traditionally marginalized groups, the incorporation of these elected officials into governing coalitions, and securing the dominance of that coalition.[24] Although not insignificant, political protest or expressing one's political voice is just one facet of political participation necessary to achieve political power.

Which brings us to today and the prominence of contemporary social movements in politics. Many believe that the recent protest movements and increased activism around such issues as gun control and racial equity are good for the country and indeed unite the country. A 2020 YouGovAmerica poll found that 58 percent of Black Americans across generations believed that activism for social change unites the country and that this unity will persist. In familiar ways, views differ on the uniting effect of recent protests, with only one-third of white Americans viewing protests as a unifying force and older white Americans seeing them as "divisive." Views also differ by political party, with 79 percent of white Republicans viewing the protests as divisive now, and 53 percent believing they will continue to divide the country.[25] These poll results align with Intravia, Piquero, and Piquero's research regarding national anthem protests in the National Football League, in which they found that Black respondents were more likely to support all types of anthem protests and also to believe that players who protest the anthem should not be disciplined by the NFL or by team owners.[26]

Despite these gaps in appreciation—generational, partisan, racial—the relevance of contemporary protests must be acknowledged. The Brookings Institution's Andrea Perry and Carl Romer assert that protests are just as important as voting—the sine qua non of democratic citizenship. "Public protests are manifestations of dissent and an expression of the urgent need to change policy. By driving media coverage, catalyzing congressional action, and shifting public opinion, nonviolent protests have been a force behind positive social change." Rather than a precursor or a lesser act of democratic engagement, they hold up protesting not only as a meaningful route for change but possibly the best route for those who are seemingly powerless. "By framing voting as the be all, end all form of engagement, we minimize protesting's power to change policy. We also ignore why people have taken to the streets in the first place: Their voices are not being heard through conventional means."[27]

Expressing one's political voice certainly is an extension of the core elements of democracy—the liberty to hold your own opinion, to petition the government, to assemble with others. A constitutional design founded on "ambition countering ambition," with multiple entry points for citizens to interject their opinion also provides the public opportunities to vent or let off steam, or as Meyers refers to it, "institutional dissent," a "way of bringing political conflict into the government in order to confine the boundaries of claims that activists might make and to invite partisans to struggle using conventional political means rather than taking up arms or opting out of the system."[28]

From the suffragists' fight for the vote to the civil rights movement to contemporary activism, there are multiple examples of the expression of political voice shifting public consciousness and influencing policy throughout American history. The research reminds us, though, to pay close attention to how well these actions represent the people and their interests. Like voting, protesting or attending city council meetings or writing letters to the editor take time and resources, and it is often those with more time and resources participating in and even benefiting from these actions. It is also worth questioning why people are protesting, and specifically, why there is a greater urge to protest today that fifty years ago. Is it, as Perry and Romer suggest, because the regular democratic mechanisms aren't working, or the people's opinion or vote isn't translating into government action? Is it due to a lack of responsiveness by elected leaders and public officials?

If that is the case, perhaps it is not enough to protest . . . perhaps more people need to consider running for public office.

SERVING IN OFFICE

It is often said that democracy is not a spectator sport—it requires getting in the game. It is a nation of "doers," then, that keeps a system of self-government authentic, with citizens taking the time not only to voice their political opinions in protests but extending themselves by serving on boards and commissions and even running for office at the local, state, and federal levels of government. Such participation not only reflects the democratic ideal, but ensures that those serving in office truly reflect the people they serve. When we look at the composition of the nation's representative bodies today, they don't look terribly representative. Yet research shows that representation matters. What would it take it encourage more underrepresented pockets of the populace to run for office and be successful, and why does it matter?

Who Represents Us in Office?

Founded over fifty years ago, the Center for American Women in Politics (CAWP) is the leading national source of scholarly research and current data about the political participation of women. CAWP's database of women elected officials includes data covering 120 years at all levels of government—the most complete data collection dedicated to tracking women's representation in office in the United States.[29] To be sure, the country has made great progress when it comes to electing women to office. When CAWP was founded in 1971, women made up only 2 percent of the U.S. Congress and 5 percent of state legislatures. Fifty years later, 27 percent of the U.S. Congress and 31 percent of state legislatures were composed of women, and the first woman, Kamala Harris, was serving as the vice president of the United States.[30] Yes, this is progress, but not parity, given that 50 percent of the American population is composed of women.[31]

The United States' racial and ethnic composition reflects the republic's nickname—a "nation of immigrants." Although the majority of the population (76%) is classified as "White alone" by the U.S. Census Bureau, this percentage drops to 60 percent when respondents are asked if they are "White alone, not Hispanic or Latino." Eighteen percent of the U.S. population is composed of those identifying as "Hispanic or Latino," 13.4 percent are estimated to be Black alone or in combination with other races, and 6 percent are Asian alone.[32] Is this diversity reflected in the nation's representative bodies? Notably, the seating of the 117th Congress in January 2021 ushered in the most diverse body of representatives in the nation's history:

- Sixty-one African American members of Congress (11.3% of the body)—fifty-eight serving in the House of Representatives and three in the Senate;
- Fifty-one Hispanic or Latino members of Congress (9% of the total membership)—forty-four in the House and seven in the Senate;
- Twenty-one members are of Asian, South Asian, or Pacific Islander ancestry (3.9% of the total membership)— nineteen in the House and two in the Senate;
- Five Native American or Native Hawaiian members (0.9% of the total congressional membership).

These data reflect improved representation of the nation's racial and ethnic diversity. In the 1985–1986 Congress, there were only twenty-one African American members (all serving in the House of Representatives). In 1961–1962, there were only four African Americans serving in Congress. There have been similar increases in Hispanic or Latino representation—in 1985–1986, only fourteen members of Congress were Hispanic or Latino, and they were all male. In that same Congress, only five members of the House and two senators were of Asian, South Asian, or Pacific Islander ancestry.[33] Again, increased racial and ethnic diversity is progress. Still, gaps remain, with the Hispanic or Latino population particularly underrepresented at the highest levels of government.

Another indicator worthy of consideration is generational representation. At this moment, young adults of the Millennial generation and Generation Z compose the largest portion of the American populace. Baby Boomers, once the largest generation in American history at 77 million people, have now been overtaken in size by Millennials (those born between 1981 and 1996) and Generation Z (those born after 1997)—combined, Millennials and Generation Z stand at 88 million.[34] Not only do these younger generations distinguish themselves in size, but in character: the most ethnically and racially diverse generations in American history, the most educated at this stage of their lives, "digital natives" with a digital expertise that that no other age group before them possesses, civically and politically interested and inclined. Young adults also have been and will be uniquely affected by the public problems the nation is facing—from the "Great Recession" to the global pandemic and remote instruction, to gun violence in schools, to global warming, to the student loan debt crisis. In short, they should have a seat at the table. Do they?

This topic has been of particular interest to the Center for Youth Political Participation that I have directed, where the

Young Elected Leaders Project (YELP) is located. Begun in 2002, YELP collects data on the number of young adults serving in office at all levels of government, their background, their pathway to office, and their approach to leadership. When this study began, Generation X was the cohort of young adults under study, and the research team found that there were very few members of that generation serving in office, that the few who were serving were predominantly white and Christian, and that most governed as *new* elected leaders rather than *young* elected leaders.[35]

About twenty years later, the subject matter remains compelling, not only given the unique status of Millennials and Generation Z, but also given the stark contrast in age between the U.S. Congress and the rest of the population. At the time of this writing, the median age of the population is estimated to be thirty-eight years old.[36] In contrast, the median age of members of the House of Representatives at the beginning of the 117th Congress was fifty-eight years, and the average age of senators is sixty-four years.[37] Of course, Article I of the Constitution places age stipulations on congressional service—members must be twenty-five years old to serve in the House of Representatives and thirty years old to serve in the Senate. There is also good reason for members to possess enough experience to fully appreciate their role and make a meaningful contribution to the body—experience that younger Americans lack. Still, the extent to which members of Congress can fully appreciate and adequately represent younger adults has been a growing source of concern. The generational divide was quite apparent, for example, in Senate questioning of Facebook's Mark Zuckerberg in 2018, when it seemed not all members were entirely sure what the platform did or how it operated. More recently, Rebecca Traister's reporting for a 2022 *New York* article on eighty-nine-year-old Senator Dianne Feinstein raised alarms not only about the senator's ability to represent the populace on the most pressing policy concerns but also on her cognitive faculties.[38] Much like gender and racial and ethnic background, it is worth questioning how well representative bodies can represent "the people" when generational qualities and experiences are so vastly different.

Representation

There has been a vast amount of academic literature produced on the subject of political representation—how we conceive of it, how we measure it, and how we ensure it. Needless to say, the topic is of great importance when it comes to "keeping the republic" and maintaining a representative form of democracy. Long-standing conceptions of political representation focus on the nature of the role of an elected official—are they meant to act as "trustees" or "delegates"? In simplest terms, the elected official serving as a "delegate" bases their actions on the will of their constituents, while the "trustee" acts according to what they believe is in the best interest of their constituents.

In his exploration and reexamination of the trustee/delegate typology, Andrew Rehfeld summarizes the historical conceptualization of the representative as delegate as one "who (1) aims at the good of his or her constituents, (2) as judged by his or her constituents, (3) more responsive to external sanction (election or the avoidance of legal penalties)." In contrast, the historical understanding of the trustee is "one who (1) aims at the good of the whole, (2) as judged by the representative, (3) less responsive to sanction, but acting on some form of civic virtue instead."[39] Rehfeld argues that the trustee/delegate model is too restrictive, and rather than binary, the representation model is multifaceted and even can apply to contexts beyond elected democratic representatives.

In crafting a more nuanced conceptualization of representation, Rehfeld looks to work by such scholars as Jane Mansbridge and Hannah Pitkin. It was Pitkin's classic 1967 work that led scholars to understand representation as composed of three interrelated dimensions: descriptive, symbolic, and substantive representation. *Descriptive* representation relates to the extent to which a representative possesses the same qualities or background as those they are representing. Discussions earlier about the demographic composition of the U.S. Congress in relation to the demographic composition of the populace reflect this dimension of representation. *Symbolic* representation relates to who a representative stands for or speaks for—the election of Delaware's Sarah McBride as the first transgender state senator might be an example of the symbolic representation of a historically marginalized portion of the populace. *Substantive* representation refers to the degree to which elected officials act on behalf of or in the interest of their constituents or group interests through their policy stances. An elected official who advances the interests of a heavily prevalent industry in their district or state is an example of substantive representation. Questions unresolved, though, include how these dimensions relate to one another and how they might be used to assess how well an elected official is representing their constituents.

Mansbridge's "Rethinking Representation" takes on this challenge and concludes that neither Pitkin's typology nor the trustee/delegate model adequately captures how we should think about representation. Instead, she offers a typology that includes "promissory," "anticipatory," "gyroscopic," and "surrogate" representation and urges a more multifaceted approach to assessing the quality of representation. "Conceiving of democratic legitimacy as a spectrum and not a dichotomy, one might say that the closer a system of representation comes to meeting the normative criteria for democratic aggregation and deliberation, the more that system is normatively legitimate."[40]

Rehfeld takes this argument a step further, concluding that typologies explaining the nature of an elected official's representation should consider the aims a representative should pursue (the good of the whole, or the people at large, or a particular slice), what sources of judgment decision makers should rely on (their own, or some other entity such as constituents or interest groups), and whether the representative should be more or less responsive to sanctions for their work (does an elected official risk losing reelection for their actions?). For Rehfeld, consideration of all of these factors captures the complexity of the decision making of representatives and indeed the nature of representation itself.

So where does this leave us in our understanding of representation? Like the review of academic literature on voting presented in chapter 4, it is too simplistic to assume that there is one comprehensive and definitive definition of democratic representation that is both normatively appropriate and meets the wishes and needs of constituents. For example, it is not enough to argue that Congress as a body would be more "representative" and would receive higher approval ratings from the public if it was more descriptively representative of the nation. That is not to say that descriptive representation is irrelevant to the quality of representation or to constituents. Indeed, there is plenty of research demonstrating that, to use an expression now common in the public lexicon, "representation matters."

For example, Hayes and Hibbing found in their experimental research on the symbolic benefits of descriptive and substantive representation that citizens value descriptive representation independently of substantive representation, and that the degree of descriptive representation desired by citizens is conditional on the nature of the policy being considered (such as affirmative action). In short, descriptive representation may increase the sense that decision-making processes in elected bodies—even when they don't align with the citizens' preferred policies—are fair or satisfactory.[41] Minta and Sinclair-Chapman's research on the "diversity infrastructure theory" makes a strong case that descriptive representation plays a key role in ensuring substantive representation of populations traditionally unrepresented. Using over fifty years of data from congressional hearings on civil rights and social welfare, they find that it was the presence of legislators from minority communities that kept these issues on the agenda even when the public was less interested.[42] Finally, in their study of constituency service, Lowande, Ritchie, and Lauterbach find that descriptive representation matters beyond the passage of legislation, but extends to following through with policy implementation. Specifically, they found that women, racial/ethnic minorities, and veterans are more likely to work on behalf of constituents with whom they share identities.[43] Together, this research supports the idea that "representation matters," but in ways that may not be so obvious.

To extend Mansbridge's argument, it may be more useful, then, to view representation as a "spectrum and not a dichotomy." To be sure, it is more than determining whether one should act as a trustee or delegate and under what conditions. In ways scholars are continuing to understand, electing representative bodies that demographically reflect the populace they represent also matters—in ways that are beyond symbolic and that include advancing not only policy and implementation but providing a sense of legitimacy and fairness. As Crenshaw and others' work has shown, there are shortcomings to viewing such categories as race and gender as separate and distinct when sometimes these identities intersect—often one's service in office is influenced by both race and gender working simultaneously.[44] Ensuring an electoral system that is accessible and offers a broad range of citizens an opportunity to run for office and be successful is critical to authentic representation in the United States. If we want the city councils, state legislatures, and U.S. Congresses of the future to look like the populace they represent, consideration needs to be given to pathways available to potential elected leaders today and the into the future. In short, "You can't be it if you can't see it."[45]

What does running for office look like in the United States, and what systems are in place that help some and hinder others when it comes to launching and winning an electoral campaign?

Running for Office

It would be entirely understandable if potential candidates were less than eager to run for office, given the realities of campaigning. Moreover, serving in office often seems to be a thankless job. At the time of this writing, congressional approval ratings stand at 16 percent, with a plurality of 37 percent indicating that they have "not very much" trust or confidence in the legislative branch of the federal government.[46] Only 23 percent indicated in a 2022 Gallup poll that they had "great deal or quite a lot" of confidence in the office of the president—a decrease of 15 percent from the year before.[47] Although rates of trust in state and local government remain higher than for the federal government, even rates of trust in state and local governments' ability to handle problems has declined in recent years.[48]

Then, of course, there's the cost of running for office and the hours of fundraising that must take place to launch a viable campaign. The organization Open Secrets, a nonpartisan research group studying campaign spending, reported that the average winning House candidate in 2020 spent $2,354,620 and the average Senate candidate spent $27,157,566. The most expensive House campaign that year, for Republican Steve Scalise from Louisiana, spent $32,830,607. On the Senate side,

Georgia Democrat Jon Ossoff's campaign was the cycle's most expensive at a whopping $149,298,378.[49]

For nonincumbents running for office, the process is even more daunting. When it comes to raising money, incumbents are at a tremendous advantage, with the average Senate incumbent raising over $15,316,869 compared to an average of $887,339 for challengers and $1,989,681 for the average candidate for an open seat in the Senate. Similar advantages are enjoyed by House incumbents—for the 2021–2022 election cycle, the average House incumbent raised $1,818,643, while the average House challenger raised $191,331 and the average open-seat candidate raised $340,354.[50] Raising money is not the only advantage incumbents have when it comes to running for office; in many ways, their superiority in raising money reflects the many institutional advantages incumbency enjoys that make it difficult for challengers to be successful.

Scholars have detailed the many structural features of congressional officeholding that put incumbents at a distinct advantage and make it so difficult for newcomers to unseat them. Incumbents' position in office provides a multitude of opportunities to serve their constituents' interests and deliver them direct benefits, to secure office and staff resources that allow for travel to their districts and communication with constituents, and to enhance their name recognition and familiarity. Combined, these advantages are often a successful way to scare away challengers. As Gary Jacobson writes, "If an incumbent can convince potentially formidable opponents and people who control campaign resources that he or she is invincible, he or she is likely to avoid a serious challenge and so will be invincible—as long as the impression holds."[51]

The lack of descriptive representation in elected office is all the more understandable, then, given the power of incumbency. Research paired with practical efforts to build the capacity of candidates offers a meaningful route, though, for enhancing the success of challengers and shifting the demographics of elected bodies so they reflect the populace they represent. Indeed, there is value in understanding the evidence-based logic of campaigning and applying it to one's own potential campaigns. As Burton, Miller, and Shea's *Campaign Craft* asserts in linking the theoretical understanding with the practical realities of campaigning, such an exercise serves to "clear away some of the mystery surrounding a sometimes enigmatic, frequently exasperating, and always intriguing aspect of American politics."[52] The research highlights the barriers thwarting nonincumbents' electoral success and can inform efforts to prepare and equip potential candidates.

For example, the Center for American Women and Politics has produced meaningful scholarship over its more than fifty years on the factors that hamper the success of women candidates and the steps necessary to make their candidacies successful. As Dittmar, Sanbonmatsu, and Carroll found in their interviews of women serving in Congress, securing a seat in office often is viewed by women elected officials as far more challenging than serving. One member of Congress stated, "Being here in Congress is not as hard as it was to get here."[53] From having to work twice as hard to raise money as men do; to often lacking the networks of institutional support necessary to launch a campaign; to the gender differences they face regarding their family and marital status, women face unique obstacles when it comes to running for office, and sometimes these challenges are intersectional, with women of color uniquely affected.[54] In response, CAWP's Ready to Run® program, created in New Jersey and now a national program, provides nonpartisan training to encourage women to run for office and position themselves for appointive office. The trainings include instruction on fundraising, navigating political party structures, working with the media, building a team of volunteers, and getting out the vote.[55]

Similar efforts have been geared toward supporting and encouraging first- and second-generation Americans as they put themselves in positions to be successful in electoral campaigns. New American Leaders' training Ready to Lead® is centered around the idea of "the immigrant experience as an asset in civic leadership." The program offers participants the training and encouragement to "embrace one's heritage to become a successful candidate."[56] On the Rutgers University campus, the Center for Youth Political Participation Program has enhanced research on young elected leaders with the program RU Running—a campaign training for college students who think they might want to run for office one day, or at least want to learn the nuts and bolts of working on a campaign.[57] In addition to these nonpartisan programs, there are numerous efforts on the ideological left and right geared toward recruiting and equipping candidates for office.

As we think about the expectations of active citizenship, running for office usually is ranked quite low in the list of

Figure 8. Elizabeth Cady Stanton and Susan B. Anthony. Stanton was the first woman to run for the House of Representatives. Courtesy of the National Portrait Gallery, Smithsonian Institution.

possibilities for most—well behind such behaviors as voting or speaking out about a cause we believe in. Daunting as it may seem, serving in public office at least deserves consideration, though. When we think about the numerous decisions being made by those serving in office at the local, state, and

federal levels and the effects they have on our everyday lives—
from the quality of our roads, to property taxes, to environ-
mental policy—it is worth asking the question *am I being well
represented?* If not, *am I willing to run for office and serve?*

Theodore Roosevelt, the twenty-sixth president of the
United States, lived a life that exemplified active citizenship.
Born in 1858, Roosevelt's extensive public service included
serving as a lieutenant colonel in the Spanish-American war,
governor of New York, and president of the United States at
the age of forty-three.[58] A man of many interests and passions,
conservation being one of them, Roosevelt spoke and wrote a
great deal about citizenship. In one of his more famous
speeches, entitled "Citizenship in a Republic," Roosevelt
famously characterized democratic citizenship as one of effort
and action—not sitting on the sidelines.

> It is not the critic who counts; not the man who points out
> how the strong man stumbles or where the doer of deeds
> could have done better. The credit belongs to the man who
> is actually in the arena, whose face is marred by dust and
> sweat and blood; who strives valiantly; who errs, who
> comes short again and again, because there is no effort
> without error and shortcoming; but who does actually
> strive to do the deeds; who know the great enthusiasms, the
> great devotions; who spends himself in a worthy cause; who
> at best knows in the end the triumph of high achievement,
> and who at the worst, if he fails, at least fails while doing
> greatly, so that his place shall never be with those cold and
> timid souls who neither know victory nor defeat.[59]

So "keeping the republic" sometimes requires a willingness to get in the arena.

GETTING INVOLVED

Last, but not necessarily of least importance when it comes to the "job of citizenship," is volunteering, being an active member of our community. The health and vitality of democracies traditionally has been understood to stem from civic life or "civil society," defined by Peter Levine as "an array of institutions in which citizens can inform themselves, deliberate, and address public problems."[60] From Aristotle's conception of community to Tocqueville's depiction of the United States as a nation of joiners, self-government has been seen as an extension of the citizenry's interest and involvement in the day-to-day life of our towns and cities. To round out this consideration of what it means to act like a democratic citizen, I will explore the nature of this connection, outline current rates of community involvement among Americans, and conclude by highlighting what we can do to revive and maintain that sense of public service essential to "keeping the republic."

Connecting Civic Life to Democracy

Much of democratic thought has looked to relationships or associations as building blocks of self-government. Indeed, it was in his work *Politics* that Aristotle posited the idea that societies and power structures built on relationships and networks of associations were the most desirable forms of being. "Every state is a community of some kind, and every community is established with a view to some good; for everyone acts in order to obtain that which they think is good, the state or the political community, which is the highest of all, and which embraces all the rest, aims at good in a greater degree than any other, and at the highest good."[61]

It was Tocqueville's chronicling of democracy in the United States that really originated the characterization of the American citizenry as active and vibrant and engaged in the daily life of the local community.[62] Consideration of the role of civic involvement in the health of democracies is interwoven through such classic political science scholarship as *The Civic Culture* and *Voice and Equality*. As Verba, Schlozman, and Brady argue in *Voice and Equality*, the societal and governmental structures of the United States facilitate a multitude of nonpolitical volunteering opportunities in the United States via nonpolitical organizations ranging from PTAs to local gardening clubs or sports leagues to churches and nonsecular religious organizations. These nonpolitical volunteering possibilities often serve as a route, though, to political engagement by building skills that are transferable to politics, serving as the context for recruiting participants in political activities, or even tangentially involving or intermingling with politics.[63] By not only building skills of self-government, civil society and the citizens composing it can meet public needs that can't realistically be met by a democratic regime.[64]

Rates of Volunteering

Still, liberal democracies such as the United States require an equitable civil society—one that is reflective and accessible to the populace. Like protesting and speaking out, the capacity required when it comes to volunteering, holding a leadership role in nonpolitical organizations, and supporting causes one believes in may benefit a select few and preclude the involvement of many (certainly when it comes to making financial donations). Possessing such resources as time, money, skill, and connections can be a precursor to civic engagement. Certainly, the 1995 scholarship in *Voice and Equality* shows that broad numbers of Americans engage in nonpolitical work or are involved in some capacity in the civil society—from affiliating with nonpolitical organizations, to attending church regularly, to making donations to church or charitable donations—and that nonpolitical activity exceeds and really takes precedence over political activity.[65]

Recent data from the Current Population Survey (CPS) analyzed by the AmeriCorps Office of Research and Evaluation underscores the high rates of involvement in civic life today, with an estimated 30 percent of Americans indicating that they had volunteered for an organization or association in the previous year, amounting to an estimate of 5.8 billion hours of service (an estimated economic value of $147 billion). These recent data also highlight gaps in rates of volunteering along gender, income, education, and racial and ethnic lines:

- One-third of women volunteered compared to one-quarter of men;
- Thirty-two percent of whites volunteered compared to 25 percent of those of another race;

- Middle-age Americans (Generation X) volunteered at rates higher than other generations.[66]

Differences in rates of volunteering for organizations or associations only increase when educational attainment and income levels are included, suggesting the inaccessibility of these forms of engagement for many. At the same time, these differences also suggest that measuring civic involvement via involvement in organizations or associations is an insufficient accounting of Americans' community engagement. As AmeriCorps's Laura Hanson Schlachter points out, "These types of patterns raise broader questions about the complex drivers of variation in organization-based volunteering rates and the distinction between volunteering and professional development."[67]

Although those with higher incomes are more likely to participate in nonpolitical activities and donate more than those with lower income, *Voice and Equality* concluded that the differences are less stark in civic life than in political life—suggesting that there are more opportunities and possibilities for equity in the civic society. Encouraging recent trends in youth engagement in voting and activism also are evident in community engagement. The Center for Information and Research on Civic Learning and Engagement shows that young women of color in particular are taking an interest in their communities and becoming active participants in civic life:

- Eighty-seven percent of Latina women and 83 percent of Black women agreed or strongly agreed with the statement

"It is my responsibility to get involved and make things better for my society";

- Sixty-five percent of Asian women and 53 percent of Black women reported having worked with others to address a community issue;
- Sixty-five percent of Latina women and 63 percent of Asian women indicate that they have acted to reduce the unfair treatment of people of color in their community.[68]

Instilling a Sense of Service

Like all other forms of democratic citizenship, from voting to running for office, building the capacity to engage in public service is elemental. Public service is a democratic mindset and inclination that needs to be taught and encouraged, and this sort of work is being done for schoolchildren, college students, and lifelong learners all across the country. One way educators are instilling a sense of public spirit is through service-learning—an active learning approach to teaching civic engagement that engages students in the activities of their community. More than volunteering, service-learning activities are interwoven into course curriculums and reflect learning objectives with numerous opportunities for reflection and group discussion. As Alison Rios Millett McCartney explains, "service-learning seeks to empower students through building the necessary knowledge, skills, and experiences to become capable, effective, and successful citizens."[69]

Service-learning has become a prominent approach to teaching civic engagement. It is a pedagogy that has generated a good deal of scholarship and has been advanced by national organizations—from disciplinary ones such as the American Political Science Association and the National Council for the Social Studies, to interdisciplinary ones such as Campus Compact. Well-known national initiatives such as Teach for America stem from this approach—one that aims to not only meet the needs of community members experiencing economic and social challenges but also fosters civic competencies in those meeting those needs.[70] The newly launched Rutgers Summer Service Internship initiative on my campus has a similar aim—to involve students in public service internships; ground their experiences in coursework; and use the immersive experience to teach the connections between communities and political systems, to help students understand and learn from differences, and to instill a civic ethos.[71]

These structured service opportunities are not restricted to the classroom or college campus. Initiatives such as AmeriCorps, Everyday Democracy, and Citizen University all offer meaningful routes for connecting with each other and participating directly in the civic life of our communities.[72] Everyday Democracy, for example, facilitates the organization of diverse groups at the community level to engage in dialogue on public problems facing their community and act collaboratively to address these problems. Citizen University also serves as an organizing force (through gatherings and workshops) built around strengthening civic culture with the aim of "sparking new ways of thinking about citizenship, deepening the resolve to take responsibility, and rekindling faith in our democracy and one another."[73]

This chapter is by no means an exhaustive list of the actions individuals and bodies of individuals can pursue to hold government accountable. For example, civil disobedience historically has served as a powerful nonviolent weapon for raising awareness and sparking political change in the United States and worldwide. From Henry David Thoreau's refusal to pay taxes to protest the institution of slavery and America's war with Mexico, to Rosa Parks's refusal to give up her bus seat for a white passenger, such public and principled acts of conscientious law breaking can be effective methods of political action.[74] Social entrepreneurship or crafting innovative solutions to critical social needs is another way individuals might act to address public problems without making direct use of existing political institutions.[75] Like civil disobedience, doggedly pursuing resourceful and results-oriented solutions via social entrepreneurship can shift public consciousness, spark social change, and reflect the political power of the people.

For reasons outlined earlier, shoring up our civil society is intricately linked to democracy's health and longevity. Whether public service is instilled formally in the classroom or via a nonprofit organization or comes more naturally or organically, these efforts play a vital role not only in developing the skills of self-government, but in keeping the citizenry more in tune with the needs of their community and more aware of how well these needs are being met by those representing us in office. Together, expressing our political voice, serving in office, and serving in our communities reflect the sort of accountability necessary in a republic. As citizens electing a body of individuals to represent us, our job is to keep watch and hold officials accountable for their actions or inactions.

Again, democracy is not a spectator sport—we also must "get in the arena." Whether it's showing up to serve on a committee or run for office or simply come together with our community to engage and tackle local issues, we must hold ourselves accountable as citizens—ensuring we're doing all we can to "keep the republic." To borrow a phrase commonly heard at recent protests and demonstrations, "This is what democracy looks like."

CHAPTER 6

It Depends on Us

As Ed Folsom highlights in his introduction to Walt Whitman's classic essay *Democratic Vistas*, Whitman's essay is regarded more for its title than the content of the essay itself. Folsom writes that the phrase "democratic vistas" "has become a kind of shorthand phrase for the distinctly American sense that the nation's egalitarian fulfillment is always just on the horizon, the faith that our founding ideals are not behind us but always still ahead of us, in our perpetually beckoning future."[1] Certainly the spirit contained in the title reflects the importance I have placed in this book on the role of democratic inspiration. As Folsom points out, though, even though Whitman wrote *Democratic Vistas* in Washington, D.C., around the time of the end of the end of the Civil War and the passage of the Thirteenth and Fourteenth Amendments to the U.S. Constitution, the author makes no reference to the institution of slavery or equality of the formerly enslaved persons in his musings.[2] Like the country he writes about, then, Whitman exemplifies the contradictions we see within our democratic thinking and citizenship.

As I asserted at the outset, the United States seems to be at an inflection point—one that could lead us all closer to the ideals we claim to embody or further away. We hear it in our discourse, we witness it in our campaigns and elections, we see it in our streets and in our communities. Even the way we think about what it means to be a democratic citizen might serve as a turning point in our nation's trajectory as we ask ourselves what has American democracy looked like throughout our history, what does it look like now, and what will it look like in the future? The questions we grapple with today bring to mind the distinction Tocqueville made nearly 200 years ago in contrasting conceptions of patriotism—the "instinctive" sort that's reverential and ardent but resistant to critical reflection, and the "well-considered" type that is less passionate and more thoughtful (referenced in chapter 2). It is fair to say that these dueling versions of patriotism are playing out today in policy debates about civic education. Florida, for example, has taken steps to revamp its civic education curriculum in ways that emphasize patriotism and exceptionalism but limit opportunities for vigorous class discussion and experiential learning—with critics charging that the content is laden with Christian and ideologically conservative themes.[3]

The goal of this book has been to highlight the multiple facets of democratic citizenship, to identify and explore American democracy's sometimes competing values and ideals as well as the points of resonance and unity, and to bridge the gap in understanding between the theoretical and the practical by highlighting and translating relevant scholarship on demo-cratic participation. I will round out this text by sharing a moment in literary history that I came across in researching this book that I believe illuminates the core themes of *To Keep the Republic*. It is a story shared by the Walt Whitman Associa-tion located in Camden, New Jersey, about the decision of Langston Hughes, leading poet of the Harlem Renaissance, to speak at the Walt Whitman House and Hughes's vocal defense of Whitman later in his life. The vignette highlights what it means to confront the failings of human beings, whether they are artists or statesmen, yet continue to pursue the trail they blazed and the aspirations they inspired. For although nonpartisan, this book is about the value of *keeping the repub-lic*. My hope is that not only the reflection on Whitman and Hughes but all of the material presented in this text will kindle a recognition that the success of the "democratic experiment" is neither one-dimensional nor guaranteed and that ultimately, it depends on the people who compose it to "keep the republic."

A LITERARY KINSHIP
Walt Whitman

The so-called "bard of democracy," Walt Whitman was an influential poet whose work has contributed mightily to our collective depiction of American democracy—one that celebrates the individual and envisions an equitable and pluralistic democracy. Born on May 31, 1819, on Long Island, New York, Whitman was raised in a working-class home of first-generation Americans who, as Ed Folsom and

Kenneth M. Price note, "were born in the newly formed United States and grew up assuming the stable existence of the new country."[4] The second of nine children, the farmhouse in which he was born was constructed by his father Walt Whitman Sr.—it's now a State Historic Site listed on the National Register of Historic Places.[5]

Later moving to Brooklyn, Whitman began to work at the age of eleven for an attorney, and then forged his career as a writer by beginning an apprenticeship in 1831 with the *Long Island Patriot*, described as a "liberal, working-class newspaper."[6] After time spent as a schoolteacher, Whitman began to build a career as a journalist and held editorial positions for various newspapers in Long Island, New York City, and New Orleans. This time as a journalist proved to be influential in his career as a poet, write Folsom and Price. "These early years on his own in Brooklyn and New York remained a formative influence on his writing, for it was during this time that he developed the habit of close observation of the ever-shifting panorama of the city, and a great deal of his journalism, poetry, and prose came to focus on catalogs of urban life and the history of New York City, Brooklyn, and Long Island."[7]

Whitman's collective body of writing grew, then, from these roots, shaping our depiction of him as the voice not of aristocratic Europe but of a democratic United States—one that celebrates the individual, sees beauty in the work of everyday laborers, and champions the downtrodden. These themes come through not only in *Democratic Vistas* but in countless other poems—mostly those contained in a succession of editions of *Leaves of Grass* (first published in 1855 as a collection of twelve long poems, with several subsequent editions published up until Whitman's death in 1892). From "I Hear America Singing" (referenced in chapter 2) to "Song of Myself" to "Song of the Open Road" to "I Sing the Body Electric," this body of poetry not only marked a dramatically new form of verse but also shaped his reputation as a voice of liberty, individuality, and equity.

On issues surrounding racial equality, though, Whitman's views were at best complicated. As George Hutchinson and David Drews write, "the truth is that Whitman in person largely, though confusedly and idiosyncratically, internalized typical white racial attitudes of his time, place, and class. The poet not only grew up in a racist environment, a descendant of slaveowners, but also followed (without always embracing) forms of 'ethnological science' that throughout the nineteenth century presented racist arguments contradicting the poet's egalitarian principles."[8] Although he opposed slavery, his motivations often seemed rooted less in egalitarianism and more in white nationalism. In contradiction, there are expressions in his writing suggesting that he viewed formerly enslaved African Americans as equal members of the democratic republic.

The contrasts between Whitman's personal views and the tenor of his writing are not newly discovered nor a reflection solely of a contemporary consciousness. Deshae Lott writes that Whitman's resistance to extending the right to vote to African American men damaged his friendship with supporter William O'Connor.[9] Indeed, his views on race were at odds with many of his contemporary supporters, most of

Figure 9. Walt Whitman. Photograph by George C. Cox, 1887.
Courtesy of the Library of Congress.

whom were abolitionists and anti-racist. All of this, then,
makes Langston Hughes's willingness to speak at the Whitman House thirty-five years after Whitman's death and his
defense of Whitman even more interesting.

Langston Hughes

As Pauline Miller writes in her essay published in *Conversations*, the newsletter of the Walt Whitman Association, March

Figure 10. The Walt Whitman House, 328 Mickle Street, Camden, New Jersey. Source: Public domain.

was a notable month for those early champions of Walt Whitman's legacy advocating to preserve the Whitman home on Mickle Street in Camden, New Jersey—the only home he ever owned. March 27, 1892, was the date of Whitman's death, and so an event held at the Whitman House on March 1, 1927, would have been meaningful. This event, though, was all the more meaningful because it would feature remarks by the leading poet of the Harlem Renaissance, Langston Hughes.

Born in 1902, Langston Hughes was a poet as well as a novelist, essayist, and writer of short stories and essays. He was a leading figure of the Harlem Renaissance—a period of great cultural, literary, and intellectual advances among African American communities. Hughes developed a style that aimed to capture and celebrate the everyday and authentic life of

African Americans. Jazz was in its ascendency in the United States at that time and was reflected in the rhythm and cadence of Hughes's poetry.[10] As Hughes expressed, "Most of my own poems are racial in theme and treatment, derived from the life I know. In many of them I try to grasp and hold some of the meanings and rhythms of jazz."[11]

Out of his body of poetry, "Let America Be America Again" (referenced in chapter 2) and "I, Too" have emerged as some of the most resonant, capturing both the contradictions and hypocrisies of America as well as its promise and possibility for redemption. They also reflect the strong literary kinship between Hughes and Walt Whitman. Indeed, "I, Too," written in 1926, is seen as a response to Whitman's joyful "I Hear America Singing."

Hughes and the Legacy of Whitman

It is notable, then, that, at the age of twenty-five, Hughes was invited to speak at the Walt Whitman House and that he accepted the invitation to join in a celebration of Whitman's life and work. As Pauline Miller writes, the occasion served as "a bridge between Whitman's philosophy and an African American audience,"[12] prompting New Jersey's *Evening Courier* to mark the event in this way: "If old Walt Whitman, atop Mount Olympus, looked down upon his Mickle street house Tuesday night, he must have felt that all his songs of equality had not been wasted upon a scurrying, restless world."[13] Although quite generous to Whitman, this sentiment has some merit in that Hughes promised to take the aspirations contained in Whitman's poetry (hollow as

they may have been) and fill them with a meaning authentic
to all Americans.

Later in his life, Hughes defended Whitman and his reputation as a poet of democracy even in the face of significant
criticism. In a column published in the *Chicago Defender* on
the 4th of July in 1953, Hughes wrote, "But more than a mere
pioneer in style, Whitman was a pioneer in the expression of
poetry of the basic precepts of American democracy as applying to everyone, white or black."[14] Hughes went on to declare,
"His 'Leaves of Grass' contains the greatest poetic statements
of the real meaning of democracy ever made on our shores."
As Miller notes in *Conversations*, readers took issue with
Hughes's declaration, and Professor Lorenzo D. Turner
encouraged readers to look beyond the famed *Leaves of Grass*
to Whitman's other writings. Turner's assessment led him to
conclude that Whitman was no friend to African Americans
and indeed that he "thought they were inferior to other human
beings."[15]

Hughes did not waver in his support of Whitman, declaring that *Leaves of Grass* is a book that all "should read and
remember, for its heart and essence are decency and democracy, friendship and love for every human being." In this same
column, entitled "Like Whitman, Great Artists Are Not
Always Great People," Hughes confronts the conundrum of
appreciating the spirit, the ideals, the beauty contained in a
piece of art—whether it is a poem, or a song, or a play—but
disliking the lifestyle or the behavior or the beliefs of the
artist behind the work. Hughes reminds the reader that artists
are in fact humans. "Great people, so long as they are people,

are not gods. They are mortal human beings, subjected to all the currents and evils, sins and stupidities of their times." Despite their shortcomings, their art blazes a trail for others to follow. "But they have left, at their flaming best, a great light for others, burning even brighter perhaps from the embers of their own personal failures." For Hughes, this holds true not just for the bard of democracy but even American democracy's author himself. "If . . . Whitman sometimes contradicted his own highest ideals—just as Thomas Jefferson did by owning slaves yet writing about liberty—it is the best of him that we choose to keep and cherish, not his worst."[16]

This, then, is how Hughes dealt with the quandary of appreciating the work of Whitman and its celebration of liberty and equality in light of the poet's numerous pronouncements undermining these sentiments—by recognizing the failings of humans but separating them from their work and dissuading us from abandoning the art because of the artist's failings. More importantly, though, Hughes addressed the quandary by using his own poetry and even the inspiration from Whitman to give voice to the incongruences between the ideals and realities of the human condition and the democratic experiment. In doing so, Hughes took the spirit of "the bard of democracy" and made it more authentic and more applicable to "we the people."

"To Keep the Republic"

It is risky, of course, to extend the discrete example of Walt Whitman and Langston Hughes documented above too

Figure 11. Portrait of Langston Hughes by Carl Van Vechten, February 29, 1936. Courtesy of the Library of Congress.

broadly or to apply it too loosely to the state of American democracy today. Yes, choosing to "keep and cherish" the best and not the worst of the nation's history offers a path, but that path may not always be straight, even, or easy to tread. It's also incumbent upon us to recognize and remember the origins of American's democratic path—both the awe-inspiring and the shameful.

Like democracy itself, the job of democratic citizenship is multifaceted, complicated, and full-time. With this book, I have offered a template for that job—one that captures its complexity, is rooted in reality, but that has the aspirational in its sights. Most importantly, my hope is that this template responds to the call to action that went out from Barbara Jordan nearly fifty years ago (referenced in chapter 1)—that it sparks the "willingness of each of us to share in the responsibility for upholding the common good," and that it might encourage us to be "willing to participate in shaping the future of this nation."[17] Again, the democratic republic that emerged from the Constitutional Convention in 1787 suggests not only a way to organize a government but a way to organize ourselves—so keeping it depends upon us.

It depends upon us *thinking like democratic citizens*. Democratic citizenship is rooted less in a set of actions than in the shared set of values and norms undergirding these actions—a set of values and norms that transcend partisan affiliation, are vibrant not just in theory but also in reality, and acknowledges when these ideals have not been met. It is rooted in a mutually agreed-upon democratic code that values not only the free exercise of our innate rights but equitable access to the full enjoyment of these rights across the populace. Democratic citizenship stems from a shared belief that there is value in a diversity of backgrounds, beliefs, interests, and fair competition between these "factions," and that a system of "ambition countering ambition" offers a route for compromise and outcomes that benefit the common good. As democratic citizens, our actions are guided by popular will, but also respect for the rights of the minority and the protection of the dispassionate rule of law.

It depends upon us *talking like democratic citizens* "to keep the republic." Democratic citizenship entails bringing the ideals and values of democracy into our everyday practices—even simply in our interactions with each other. As we hold our elected officials accountable, citizenship entails holding ourselves accountable: Are we rooting our opinions in fact or fiction, are we engaging in discussions with those we disagree with or are we instinctively demonizing them? Are we willing to expose ourselves to ideas we vehemently oppose in an effort to understand? Are we willing to recognize the difference between conflicting views and dehumanizing speech and aim for authentic civility? Systems of self-government such as the United States' are so interwoven with our relationships with each other—even in the ways we talk to each other in the neighborhood, in the classroom, and in the workplace.

It depends upon us *voting—and helping others vote—like democratic citizens*. It is fundamental, of course, that democratic republics require an active and consistently participative electorate who show up for each election, providing the legitimacy necessary in a system of representative government.

Equally fundamental, though, to democratic citizenship is enabling others to vote—acknowledging gaps in participation and their implications, recognizing the barriers that keep large segments of the populace from the polls, and following the data when it comes to advancing necessary structural changes to ensure an electorate that reflects the population.

Finally, it depends upon us *acting like democratic citizens— speaking up, pitching in, and even going "into the arena"* to keep the republic. It's become a cliché to claim that democracy "is not a spectator sport," but there is truth to the idea that self-government requires our consistent attention—beyond campaign season. It takes a willingness to hold elected officials accountable by following their actions as our representatives and speaking out when the moment calls for it, to involve ourselves in the everyday life of our community, and to be willing to step up and seek civic and political leadership positions. Such year-round involvement also requires a willingness to look around the proverbial table and acknowledge who has a seat at the table and who doesn't—which voices are being heard and which aren't. It depends on us to make sure that this representative democracy is representative.

In the end, then, it doesn't matter if Benjamin Franklin really uttered the words "A republic, if you can keep it." Indeed, it might just be a myth worth believing at a time when so much that the nation has witnessed in recent history has seemed unbelievable and suggestive of a democracy in decline—from violent mobs attacking the Capitol in the hopes of derailing the outcome of an election, to rates of trust in government officials plummeting. On the other hand, who could have believed that in the midst of a global pandemic and a terribly divisive election, Americans would turn out in record numbers to vote in 2020 or that some 160 years after the Emancipation Proclamation, an African American woman would be sworn in as a justice on the Supreme Court? It is the promise contained in the "truths" we hold to be "self-evident" that compels us, then, to play our part in bringing them to fruition, creating better versions of democracy, and *hopefully*, keep the republic.

Further Reading

To Keep the Republic in many ways reflects my thinking and teaching about democratic citizenship throughout my professional career. As such, the text is peppered with references to academic scholarship (both classic and contemporary) as well as broadly accessible publications and works of literature. If readers find themselves wanting to explore the topics contained in this book further, this final section highlights works that I think are particularly informative or thought-provoking as we consider what it takes to be a democratic citizen today.

The underlying current of *To Keep the Republic* considers what American democracy is and what American democracy could be—its shortcomings and its promise. Books already referenced in the text, including Anne Applebaum's *Twilight of Democracy: The Seductive Lure of Authoritarianism* and Levitsky and Ziblatt's *How Democracies Die*, are meaningful for contextualizing the state of the nation's democracy and current red flags. Not coincidentally perhaps, conversations about the fragility of American democracy are taking place at a time when the nation has been forced to confront and grapple with inherent inequities in the democratic experience. On this topic, I found Clint Smith's *How the Word Is Passed: A Reckoning with the History of Slavery across America* particularly resonant at this moment. A chronicle of Smith's travel to monuments around the country, the author offers a narrative of how various historical landmarks (from Monticello to the Blandford Cemetery for Confederate soldiers) have either productively addressed and honestly acknowledged the institution of slavery in American history or have ignored or inaccurately accounted for it. With his reflections, Smith challenges his readers to consider how the way in which we tell our American story and memorialize our history makes an impression on our way of thinking and might explain the way we live our lives today. More importantly, the exercise offers a path for the future: "in order for our country to collectively move forward, it is not enough to have a patchwork of places that are honest about the history while being surrounded by other spaces that undermine it. It must be a collective endeavor to learn and confront the story of slavery and how it shaped the world we live in today."[1]

As *To Keep the Republic* contends, our ability to talk to one another and productively engage in difficult conversations plays a meaningful role in our ability to govern ourselves. A few texts that students utilize in the course I co-created and continue to teach, "Talking Politics: Disagreeing without Being Disagreeable" (referenced in chapter 3), offer insights into some of the core skills needed to have such conversations. Sherry Turkle's *Reclaiming Conversation: The Power of Talk in a*

Digital Age makes a case for what is lost in human connection when conversations take place in texts and emails, and what is to be gained by face-to-face communication. These evidence-based reminders encourage us to engage in the active listening needed in conversation.

Perspective-taking is another core skill of coming together in conversations—especially challenging ones. Mahzarin R. Banaji and Anthony Greenwald's *Blindspot: Hidden Biases of Good People* demonstrates how pervasive inherent biases are and how we might identify and combat them. Our ability to have difficult conversations often requires empathy, or at least an ability to see the humanity in each other. In an essay centered around the "Little Rock Nine" and the civil rights movement, Danielle Allen takes up this theme and offers a reflection on the importance of political friendship in *Talking to Strangers: Anxieties of Citizenship since Brown v. Board of Education.*

"Voting like a democratic citizen" is fully explored in chapter 4, and a number of fundamental readings are offered that explore the factors that influence voting behavior in the United States. As the chapter shows, the way we vote in the United States goes a long way in explaining how many of us vote and who votes. Recent interesting publications, then, deal with how we might vote better or creative approaches to rethinking the voting process and, hopefully, improving democracy. E. J. Dionne and Miles Rapoport's *100% Democracy: The Case for Universal Voting* offers a bold proposal for American electoral process—requiring Americans to vote. Much like paying taxes and serving on a jury, the authors offer global models for how the United States might boost voter turnout by mandating it. Another thought-provoking publication is Lee Drutman's *Breaking the Two-Party Doom Loop: The Case for Multiparty Democracy in America*. Drutman examines the role America's two-party system has played in our current state of politics—from toxic interactions to legislative impasse—and makes an argument that a multiparty system is not only needed in the United States but attainable through electoral reform.

A concluding theme of *To Keep the Republic* is that getting involved in public problem solving through speaking out, running for office, and participating in our communities is also an essential element of democratic citizenship. Useful texts that might serve as "how to guides" to engage in such work include *America, the Owner's Manual: You Can Fight City Hall—and Win* and *America, the Owner's Manual: Making Government Work for You* by former U.S. Senator Bob Graham and Chris Hand. Written from the perspective of a former lawmaker who knows "how the system works," these texts offer accessible blueprints for how citizens can identify where to direct their problem-solving efforts and the most effective tactics for engaging with the political process to effect meaningful change. Like this text, Graham and Hand see such civic engagement as part and parcel of democratic citizenship.

For those whose interest in Walt Whitman has been piqued by this text, Ed Folsom is the foremost authority, and the Walt Whitman Archive that he edits with Matt Cohen and Kenneth M. Price is replete with scholarship on Whitman's life and work.[2] Finally, if you find yourself near Camden, New

Jersey, make time to visit the Walt Whitman House.[3] The home in which he died, Whitman's spirit runs through the intimate house and the many original artifacts within it. Even more, it offers an opportunity not only to examine the work and legacy of the so-called "bard of democracy," but to reexamine ourselves and our connection to the republic we're trying to keep.

Acknowledgments

Although writing is a very solitary process, preparing a manuscript and getting a book to print requires support, expertise, and encouragement. I've been fortunate to be on the receiving end of all of the above and want to acknowledge those who've helped me along the way.

I'm grateful to Peter Mickulas of Rutgers University Press for reaching out to me and encouraging me to submit a proposal. As the manuscript has come together, I've appreciated the guidance he's provided and the support of the team at Rutgers University Press who've taken my ideas and packaged them so beautifully in this text.

I've been exceedingly fortunate to spend most of my professional career at the Eagleton Institute of Politics at Rutgers University and have benefited tremendously from the leadership of the Institute over the years. In ways she may not have even been aware of, Eagleton's former director Ruth B. Mandel was an inspiration and probably my greatest professional champion. Ruth knew that this book was in the works, but sadly is not here now to see it in print. I frequently hear her in my head and feel her in the halls of the Institute and am hopeful that she'd be proud now that it's been published. John J. Farmer, who served as Eagleton's director prior to me, likewise has been a tremendous source of support and encouragement. His career in public service and great skill as a writer offer the inspiration needed to engage in the teaching of democracy at this critical moment. Colleagues, current and former, have been a source of friendship and camaraderie as we collectively have pursued our mission to link the study of the politics with the practice, and to do so under such difficult circumstances.

Thank you to the Honorable Christine Todd Whitman, former governor of New Jersey, for contributing the foreword to this book. Governor Whitman exemplifies *To Keep the Republic*'s dedication—"to teachers of democracy, in word and deed." By speaking out about the antidemocratic actions of the party she represented in office, Governor Whitman teaches all of us what it means to put country over party and engage in the "job of citizenship."

Many thanks to those who reviewed the proposal for this book as well as the resulting manuscript. Your insightful comments and helpful suggestions made this a better book, and I'm grateful for the expertise you shared.

A marvelous student with a promising future ahead of her, Sandhya Rajagopalan provided much-needed copyediting support as I was preparing the final manuscript for submission. I am extremely grateful to her for her diligence and attention to detail.

Many thanks to the docents at the Walt Whitman House in Camden, New Jersey, for welcoming my family and me for a visit in the summer of 2021—providing not only some meaningful context but also some inspiration. Special thanks to Leo Blake and Pauline Miller, author of the excellent article on Walt Whitman and Langston Hughes referenced in the final chapter of this book.

Finally, I'm grateful to my family for their love and encouragement, with special thanks to Rich, Jane, and Eddie. Although none of the many educators in my family currently teach civics, all are just the sort of model democratic citizens to whom this book is dedicated.

Notes

FOREWORD

1. Schonfeld, "Threats to Democracy Tops List of Issues Facing US."

2. Heim, "Massive Investment in Social Studies and Civics Education Proposed"; Editorial Board, "America Must Embrace Civics and History Instruction"; Allen and Carrese, "Opinion: Our Democracy Is Ailing"; Matto, "Civics Education Is the Best Way to Prevent the Next "; "America Needs History and Civics Education to Promote Unity."

PREFACE

1. The Eagleton Institute of Politics, Rutgers University, https://eagleton.rutgers.edu/what-we-do/.

2. The Center for Youth Political Participation, Eagleton Institute of Politics, https://cypp.rutgers.edu/about-cypp/.

3. See Matto et al., eds., *Teaching Civic Engagement across the Disciplines*; Matto et al., eds. *Teaching Civic Engagement Globally*; McCartney, Bennion, and Simpson, eds., *Teaching Civic Engagement: From Student to Active Citizen*. The companion website for *Teaching Civic Engagement* can be found here: https://web.apsanet.org/teachingcivicengagement/.

4. A nonpartisan resource tracking the litigation surrounding the 2020 election as well as legal considerations surrounding the conduct of elections and access to the ballot in general is States United Democracy Center, https://statesuniteddemocracy.org/.

5. A good resource for tracking state-level legislation related to the conduct of elections and access to the ballot is the National Conference of State Legislatures, https://www.ncsl.org/research/elections-and-campaigns.aspx. The Brennan Center for Justice is a nonpartisan law and policy organization with resources and analysis related to access to the vote (https://www.brennancenter.org/issues/ensure-every-american-can-vote) and securing elections (https://www.brennancenter.org/issues/defend-our-elections).

6. The International Churchill Society dates this quote from Winston S. Churchill as November 11, 1947, https://winstonchurchill.org/resources/quotes/the-worst-form-of-government/.

CHAPTER 1 — TO KEEP THE REPUBLIC

1. Brockell, "'A Republic, if You Can Keep It.'"
2. Anishanslin, "What We Get Wrong."
3. Whitman, *Democratic Vistas*, 33.
4. Freedom House, *Freedom in the World 2021.*
5. New America, "Statement of Concern."
6. In recent years, there have been a number of books written about the decline of democracy in the United States and around the world. A few include Applebaum's *Twilight of Democracy*, Levitsky and Ziblatt's *How Democracies Die*, and Przeworski's *Crises of Democracy.*
7. For data on voter turnout in the United States compared to other developed countries, see DeSilver, "Turnout Soared in 2020"; DeSilver, "In Past Elections." See the United States Election Project for data on voter turnout in the United States, http://www.electproject.org/home.
8. See United States Election Project, http://www.electproject.org/home/voter-turnout/demographics.

9. Pew Research Center, "More Now Say It's 'Stressful' to Discuss Politics."

10. Pew Research Center, "The Public, the Political System and American Democracy."

11. University of Texas at Austin, Lyndon B. Johnson School of Public Affairs, https://lbj.utexas.edu/news/2012/lbj-professor-barbara-jordans-landmark-speech-1976-democrati.

CHAPTER 2 — THINKING LIKE A DEMOCRATIC CITIZEN

1. Tocqueville, *Democracy in America*, 23–24.

2. Macedo, ed., *Democracy at Risk*, 6.

3. Macedo, ed., *Democracy at Risk*, 7.

4. McCartney, Bennion, and Simpson, eds., *Teaching Civic Engagement*, 14.

5. For more on frameworks of democratic engagement, see Colby et al., *Educating Citizens;* Matto, *Citizen Now*, chapter 3; Levine, *The Future of Democracy*; Zukin et al., *A New Engagement?*

6. Gould et al., eds., *Guardian of Democracy*.

7. Judge Learned Hand, "I Am an American Day," quoted in Liu, *Become America*, 2.

8. Tocqueville, *Democracy in America*, 493.

9. Bennett, "Ivanka Trump Calls Rioters 'Patriots.'"

10. Khavin et al., "A Day of Rage."

11. Rubin, "'There's Still Not Justice.'"

12. Ambar, *Reconsidering American Political Thought*.

13. Madison, *Federalist* No. 10, 79.

14. Allen, "Liberty, Equality Aren't Mutually Exclusive."

15. Friedman, *Free to Choose*, 148.

16. See Hardy, *The Crooked Timber of Humanity and Liberty*.

17. Allen, *Our Declaration*, 22.

18. Allen, *Our Declaration*, 269.

19. Victor, "Democracy Is an Individual Trait."

20. Madison, *Federalist* No. 10, 78.

21. Madison, *Federalist* No. 10, 77.

22. Madison, *Federalist* No. 10, 78.

23. Madison, *Federalist* No. 51, 321.

24. For more on research on pluralism, see Baumgartner and Leech, *Basic Interests*, chapter 3.

25. Madison, *Federalist* No. 10, 80.

26. Madison, *Federalist* No. 10, 82.

27. Madison, *Federalist* No. 51, 325.

28. The nature of the America's system of government also might be referred to as a "liberal democracy"—a governmental system in which sovereignty lies with the people but essential rights and freedoms are protected by a constitution. In contrast, "illiberal democracies" are those nations that are ostensibly democratic in nature but where the legitimacy of such core features as a free press or nonpartial judicial system are compromised, often in the face of authoritarian leadership. For more on liberal and illiberal democracies, see Vormann and Weinman, eds., *The Emergence of Illiberalism*; Wallace, Kundnani, and Donnelly, "The Importance of Democracy."

29. See "America's Founding Documents: The Constitution of the United States," National Archives, https://www.archives.gov/founding-docs/constitution.

30. For more, see the White House Historical Association's "The Enslaved Household of President James Madison," https://www.whitehousehistory.org/slavery-in-the-james-madison-white-house.

31. Frum, "The Founders Were Wrong about Democracy."

32. Levinson, *Our Undemocratic Constitution*, 7–8.

33. For biographical information on Barbara Jordan, see https://history.house.gov/People/Detail/16031. For information on Jordan's service on the Judiciary Committee, see https://history.house.gov/Records-and-Research/Listing/hi_008/.

34. See https://history.house.gov/Records-and-Research/Listing/hi_008/.

35. Pew Research Center, "The Public, the Political System and American Democracy," 23.

36. Pew Research Center, "The Public, the Political System and American Democracy," 29.

37. Pew Research Center, "The Public, the Political System and American Democracy," 31–32.

38. Bartels, "Ethnic Antagonism Erodes Republicans' Commitment to Democracy"; Prothro and Grigg, "Fundamental Principles of Democracy."

39. Feierherd, Lupu, and Stokes, "A Significant Minority of Americans Say They Could Support a Military Takeover."

40. Bartels, "Ethnic Antagonism Erodes Republicans' Commitment to Democracy," 1.

41. Mann and Ornstein, *It's Even Worse Than It Looks*, 30; see also chapter 2, "The Seeds of Dysfunction."

42. Charlie Dent represented Pennsylvania's 15th Congressional District in the U.S. House from 2005 to 2018. Mary Peters was secretary of transportation during the George W. Bush administration. Denver Riggleman represented Virginia's 5th Congressional District in the U.S. House from 2019 to 2021. Michael Steele is a former chairman of the Republican National Committee. Christine Todd Whitman was governor of New Jersey from 1994 to 2001.

43. Dent et al., "Opinion: The GOP Has Lost Its Way."

44. See https://www.acallforamericanrenewal.com/.

45. Pew Research Center, "Partisan Antipathy."

46. For more on "Duverger's Law," see Riker, "The Two-Party System and Duverger's Law."

47. Tocqueville, *Democracy in America*, part 2, chapter 6, "Public Spirit in the United States."

48. "Waving the flag" is my choice of words, not Tocqueville's.

49. Tocqueville, *Democracy in America*, 275.

CHAPTER 3 — TALKING LIKE A DEMOCRATIC CITIZEN

1. See *PBS News Hour*, https://www.pbs.org/newshour/nation/watch-barack-obamas-full-eulogy-for-john-mccain.

2. Pew Research Center, "Public Highly Critical of State of Political Discourse."

3. Pew Research Center, "Public Highly Critical of State of Political Discourse."

4. Van Green, "Republicans and Democrats Alike Say It's Stressful to Talk Politics."

5. See U.S. House of Representatives, https://history.house.gov/HouseRecord/Detail/15032436187.

6. For background, see *History*, https://www.history.com/this-day-in-history/protests-at-democratic-national-convention-in-chicago.

7. See *CNN*, https://www.cnn.com/2009/POLITICS/09/09/joe.wilson/.

8. See ABC's "Loud, Disruptive Health Care Town Halls," https://www.youtube.com/watch?v=w4G9RGxahTM.

9. "Donald Trump's Presidential Announcement Speech," *Time*, https://time.com/3923128/donald-trump-announcement-speech/.

10. Fact Checker Analysis, *Washington Post*, https://www.washingtonpost.com/politics/2021/01/24/trumps-false-or-misleading-claims-total-30573-over-four-years/.

11. Twitter analytics from *Trackalytics*, https://www.trackalytics.com/twitter/profile/realdonaldtrump/.

12. Pew Research Center, "Public Highly Critical of State of Political Discourse."

13. Chiacu, "Republicans Censure Cheney, Kinzinger."

14. Grey, "In Michigan, a Dress Rehearsal"; Censk, "Heavily Armed Protesters Gather Again"; Cineas, "The Insurrection Is Happening at State Capitols, Too."

15. Regarding boards of education, see Borter, Ax, and Tanfani, "School Boards Get Death Threats." Regarding boards of elections, see So, "Trump-Inspired Death Threats."

16. Chemerinsky and Gillman, *Free Speech on Campus*, ix.

17. Chemerinsky and Gillman, *Free Speech on Campus*, chapter 3.

18. Thomas, "Educating for Democracy in Undemocratic Contexts."

19. See Knight Foundation, https://knightfoundation.org/reports/free-expression-on-campus-what-college-students-think-about-first-amendment-issues; Chokshi, "What College Students Really Think about Free Speech."

20. See Thomas, "Educating for Democracy in Undemocratic Contexts."

21. Haberman and Shear, "Trump Signs Executive Order."

22. Sachs, "Steep Rise in Gag Orders."

23. Philips, "How to Talk about Politics This Thanksgiving"; Russonello, "A Thanksgiving Myth Debunked."

24. Safer, "How to Keep Politics Out of Thanksgiving 2020."

25. Tocqueville, *Democracy in America*, 283.

26. Tocqueville, *Democracy in America*, 284.

27. Tocqueville, *Democracy in America*, 285–286.

28. Zukin et al., *A New Engagement?*, 54.

29. Levine, *The Future of Democracy*, 54.

30. Thomas Jefferson to Charles Yancey," January 6, 1816, https://tjrs.monticello.org/letter/327.

31. National Taskforce on Civic Learning and Engagement, "A Crucible Moment."

32. Others who make the argument that engaging in political discourse is a core element of democratic citizenship include Bishop, *The Big Sort*; Mutz, *Hearing the Other Side*; Rojas, "Strategy versus Understanding"; Searing et al., "Public Discussion in the Deliberative System."

33. Hess, *Controversy in the Classroom*, 15.

34. Hess, *Controversy in the Classroom*, 16–22.

35. Boatright, "Introduction," 3.

36. Boatright, "Introduction," 6.

37. Laden, "Two Concepts of Civility," 9; Muddiman, "How People Perceive Political Inactivity," points out that this facet aligns with deliberation theory.

38. Laden, "Two Concepts of Civility," 12.

39. Laden, "Two Concepts of Civility," 13.

40. Laden, "Two Concepts of Civility," 12.

41. Quotes from both Gaye Theresa Johnson and Brittney Cooper; see Bates, "When Civility Is Used as a Cudgel against People of Color."

42. Muddiman, "How People Perceive Political Incivility," 40.

43. Kenski, Coe, and Rians, "Perceptions of Incivility in Public Discourse."

44. Muddiman, "How People Perceive Political Incivility," 35.

45. Levendusky and Stecula, *We Need to Talk.*

46. Campbell, "Voice in the Classroom"; McDevitt and Kiousis, "Experiments in Political Socialization"; Hess, *Controversy in the Classroom*; Hess and McAvoy, *The Political Classroom*; Rubin, *Making Citizens*; Gould et al., *Guardian of Democracy.*

47. Rubin, *Making Citizens*; Rubin, "'There's Still Not Justice.'"

48. McCartney, Bennion, and Simpson, eds., *Teaching Civic Engagement*, 9.

49. Nicholas V. Longo, Edith Manosevitch, and Timothy J. Shaffer, "Introduction," in Shaffer et al., *Deliberative Pedagogy.*

50. Mikell, "Methods Discussion and Active Learning"; Smith and Bressler, "Who Taught You to Talk Like That?"; Oros, "Let's Debate"; Panke and Stephens, "Beyond the Echo Chamber."

51. Matto and Chmielewski, "Talking Politics."

52. For the session on active listening, we utilized the exercise in "Facilitating Political Discussion": Thomas and Brimhall-Vargas, *Facilitating Political Discussions.*

53. "Our Approach," *Better Arguments*, accessed July 19, 2021, https://betterarguments.org/our-approach/.

54. "Engaging Differences: Key Principles and Best Practices," National Institute for Civil Discourse at the University of Arizona, accessed July 19, 2022, https://nicd.arizona.edu/engaging-differences -key-concepts-and-best-practices/.

55. "Welcome," *Living Room Conversations*, accessed July 19, 2022, https://livingroomconversations.org/.

56. "About Us," *The Village Square*, accessed July 19, 2022, https:// tlh.villagesquare.us/blog/about/.

CHAPTER 4 — VOTING LIKE A DEMOCRATIC CITIZEN

Epigraph: Cohen, "Representative John Lewis."

1. See YouGovAmerica, https://today.yougov.com/topics/politics /survey-results/daily/2021/06/23/060cc/1; https://docs.cdn.yougov

.com/zd4hjkpoax/tabs_HP_Voter_Fraud_20200716.pdf;   https://
today.yougov.com/topics/politics/articles-reports/2020/10/21
/america-speaks-how-do-they-feel-about-people-who-c.

2. See U.S. Census Bureau, https://www.census.gov/newsroom
/press-releases/2021/2020-presidential-election-voting-and-registra
tion-tables-now-available.html.

3. DeSilver, "Turnout Soared in 2020."

4. See Professor Michael P. McDonald's United States Election
Project for an explanation of the differences between VEP and
VAP and examples of calculations, http://www.electproject.org
/2020g.

5. See Citizen Voting-Age Population Turnout Rates by Education,
United States Election Project, http://www.electproject.org/home
/voter-turnout/demographics. Data reported are results from Census Population Survey.

6. See "2020 Presidential Election Voting and Registration Tables
Now Available," https://www.census.gov/newsroom/press-releases
/2021/2020-presidential-election-voting-and-registration-tables-now
-available.html.

7. See Citizen Voting-Age Population Turnout Rates by Race and
Ethnicity, United States Election Project, http://www.electproject.org
/home/voter-turnout/demographics. Data reported are results from
Census Population Survey.

8. See Citizen Voting-Age Population Turnout by Age, United
States Election Project, http://www.electproject.org/home/voter
-turnout/demographics. Data reported are results from Census Population Survey.

9. DeSilver, "In Past Elections, U.S. Trailed Most Developed
Countries."

10. For more information, see the ACE Electoral Knowledge Net-
work, https://aceproject.org/main/english/es/esc07a.htm.

11. Center for Information and Research on Civic Learning and
Engagement, "Election Week 2020."

12. Center for Information and Research on Civic Learning and
Engagement, "State-by-State 2020 Youth Voter Turnout."

13. The legislation, A2014, requires the Motor Vehicle Commission (MVC) to automatically register to vote any eligible person who applies for a permit, license, or ID card unless the applicant declines the automatic voter registration. New Jersey's Governor Phil Murphy signed the legislation into law on April 17, 2018.

14. Center for Information and Research on Civic Learning and Engagement, "State-by-State 2020 Youth Voter Turnout."

15. Center for Information and Research on Civic Learning and Engagement, "Half of Youth Voted in 2020."

16. Powell, "American Voter Turnout in Comparative Perspective."

17. Wehle, *What You Need to Know about Voting and Why*, 90.

18. Wehle, *What You Need to Know about Voting and Why*, 91–95.

19. For a current update on state law affecting election practices, see the National Conference of State Legislatures (NCSL) Election Legislation Database, https://www.ncsl.org/research/elections-and -campaigns/elections-legislation-database.aspx.

20. NCSL, https://www.ncsl.org/research/elections-and-campaigns /same-day-registration.aspx.

21. NCSL, https://www.ncsl.org/research/elections-and-campaigns /voter-registration-deadlines.aspx.

22. NCSL, https://www.ncsl.org/research/elections-and-campaigns /electronic-or-online-voter-registration.aspx.

23. NCSL, https://www.ncsl.org/research/elections-and-campaigns /preregistration-for-young-voters.aspx.

24. Rosenstone and Wolfinger, "The Effect of Registration Laws on Voter Turnout."

25. Kelley et al., "Registration and Voting: Putting First Things First"; Gilliam, "Influences on Voter Turnout for U. S. House Elections in Non-Presidential Years"; Rhine, "Registration Reform and Turnout Change in the American States."

26. Rosenstone and Wolfinger, "The Effect of Registration Laws on Voter Turnout"; Rosenstone and Hansen, *Mobilization, Participation, and American Democracy*; Mitchell and Wlezien, "The Impact

of Legal Constraints on Voter Registration, Turnout, and the Composition of the American Electorate"; Alvarez, Ansolabehere, and Wilson, "Election Day Voter Registration in the United States."

27. Ansolabehere and Konisky, "The Introduction of Voter Registration and Its Effect on Turnout."

28. See Squire, Wolfinger, and Glass, "Residential Mobility and Voter Turnout"; Timpone, "Structure, Behavior, and Voter Turnout in the United States."

29. NCSL, https://www.ncsl.org/research/elections-and-campaigns /early-voting-in-state-elections.aspx.

30. See Burden et al., "The Effects and Costs of Early Voting, Election Day Registration, and Same Day Registration in the 2008 Elections." See also Brians and Grofman, "Election Day Registration's Effect on U.S. Voter Turnout"; Fenster, "The Impact of Allowing Day of Registration Voting on Turnout in U.S. Elections from 1960 to 1992"; Hanmer, *Discount Voting*; Knack, "Election-Day Registration"; Highton, "Revisiting the Relationship between Educational Attainment and Political Sophistication."

31. Burden et al., "The Effects and Costs of Early Voting, Election Day Registration, and Same Day Registration in the 2008 Elections."

32. See, for example, Rosenstone and Hansen, *Mobilization, Participation, and American Democracy*; Zukin et al., *A New Engagement?*

33. For a history and explanation of establishing Election Day, see Congressional Research Service, "Election Day: Frequently Asked Questions," file:///C:/Users/19083/Desktop/R46413.pdf.

34. Wallace, Kundnani, and Donnelly, "The Importance of Democracy."

35. Brennan Center for Justice, https://www.brennancenter.org /our-work/research-reports/freedom-vote-act.

36. Wehle, *What You Need to Know about Voting and Why*, 95–96.

37. Gómez and Doherty, "Wide Partisan Divide on Whether Voting Is a Fundamental Right or a Privilege with Responsibilities."

38. See Carnegie Corporation, "Voting Rights."

39. See U.S. Senate, https://www.senate.gov/history/partydiv.htm; https://www.senate.gov/artandhistory/history/minute/Senate _Passes_Voting_Rights_Act.htm.

40. See U.S. House of Representatives, https://history.house.gov /Congressional-Overview/Profiles/89th/; https://www.history.com /topics/black-history/voting-rights-act

41. See *Shelby v. Holder*, https://www.oyez.org/cases/2012/12-96.

42. Morris et al., "Purges."

43. Weiser and Fields, "The State of Voting 2018."

44. See Carnegie Corporation, "Voting Rights."

45. See Nichols, "Closed Voting Sites Hit Minority Counties Harder for Busy Midterm Elections"; Carnegie Corporation, "Voting Rights."

46. See States United Democracy Center's Litigation Tracker: 2020 Voting Rights Cases, https://statesuniteddemocracy.org/resources /litigation-tracker-important-2020-election-law-cases/.

47. See the Select Committee to Investigate the January 6th Attack on the United States Capitol, https://january6th.house.gov/.

48. See FactCheck.org, https://www.factcheck.org/2021/11/how -many-died-as-a-result-of-capitol-riot/.

49. Analysis by States United Democracy Center on the Arizona audit concluded, "In contrast to official procedures in Arizona and best practices around the country, the Cyber Ninjas review suffers from a variety of maladies: uncompetitive contracting, a lack of impartiality and partisan balance, a faulty ballot review process, inconsistency in procedures, an unacceptably high level of error built into the process, and insufficient security." Burden and Grayson, *Report on the Cyber Ninjas Review*.

50. See States United Democracy Center, "Democracy Crisis Report Update: New Data and Trends Show the Warning Signs Have Intensified in the Last Two Months," https://statesuniteddemocracy .org/wp-content/uploads/2021/06/Democracy-Crisis-Part-II_June -10_Final_v7.pdf.

51. See Congress.Gov, https://www.congress.gov/bill/117th-congress /house-bill/4; "The House Has Passed a Bill to Restore the Voting

Rights Act," *NPR*, August 24, 2021, https://www.npr.org/2021/08/24/1030746011/house-passes-john-lewis-voting-rights-act.

52. See Congress.Gov, https://www.congress.gov/bill/117th-congress/house-bill/1/actions?q=%7B%22search%22%3A%5B%22hr1%22%2C%22hr1%22%5D%7D&r=1&s=1.

53. Pew Research Center, "Sharp Divisions on Vote Counts."

54. Pew Research Center, "Republicans and Democrats Move Further Apart."

55. Gómez and Doherty, "Wide Partisan Divide on Whether Voting Is a Fundamental Right or a Privilege with Responsibilities."

56. The intensity of partisan competition in a contest as well as voter experience also influence the measure of "voter confidence." See MIT Election Data and Science Lab, https://electionlab.mit.edu/research/voter-confidence.

57. New Jersey State Legislature, https://www.njleg.state.nj.us/our-legislature.

58. "Total Number of Registered Voters, Ballots Cast, Ballots Rejected, Percentage of Ballots Cast and the Total Number of Election Districts in New Jersey," https://www.state.nj.us/state/elections/assets/pdf/election-results/2021/2021-general-election-voter-turnout.pdf.

59. See the National Susan B. Anthony Museum and House, https://susanb.org/suffragist/#:~:text=Anthony-,Susan%20B.,to%20press%20for%20women's%20suffrage.

60. See ruvoting.rutgers.edu; vote.org.

61. See Burden et al., "The Effects and Costs of Early Voting, Election Day Registration, and Same Day Registration in the 2008 Elections."

62. Harvard Kennedy School Institute of Politics, Survey of Young Americans' Attitudes toward Politics and Public Service, https://iop.harvard.edu/sites/default/files/content/docs/Spring%202021%20Harvard%20Youth%20Poll%20topline.pdf.

63. For quotes from John Lewis, see Moyers, "John Lewis Marches On."

CHAPTER 5 — ACTING LIKE A DEMOCRATIC CITIZEN

Epigraph: Genevieve B. Earle, "The Job of Citizenship," https://thisibelieve.org/essay/16524/.

1. *This I Believe*, https://thisibelieve.org/about/.

2. "Remembering Genevieve B. Earle: The First Woman to Sit on the NYC Council," New York City Campaign Finance Board, March 12, 2019, https://www.nyccfb.info/media/blog/remembering-genevieve-b-earle-the-first-woman-to-serve-on-the-nyc-council/.

3. *This I Believe*, https://thisibelieve.org/essay/16524/.

4. https://americanhistory.si.edu/creating-icons/women%E2%80%99s-march-2017.

5. March for Our Lives, https://marchforourlives.com/mission-story/.

6. Black Lives Matter, https://blacklivesmatter.com/about/.

7. Meyer, *The Politics of Protest*, 26–27.

8. Zukin et al., *A New Engagement?*, 54.

9. Levine, *The Future of Democracy*, 51.

10. Levine, *The Future of Democracy*, 50–51.

11. Verba, Schlozman, and Brady, *Voice and Equality*, 1.

12. Verba, Schlozman, and Brady, "Introduction," in *Voice and Equality*; see appendix A for explanation of authors' sampling.

13. Verba, Schlozman, and Brady, *Voice and Equality*.

14. Gallup, "One in Three Americans Have Felt the Urge to Protest," August 24, 2018, https://news.gallup.com/poll/241634/one-three-americans-felt-urge-protest.aspx. In line with this finding, 50 percent of those surveyed in a recent YouGovAmerica poll responded yes to the question "Have you ever boycotted a business (e.g., stopped buying goods or services in protest of a business)?" https://today.yougov.com/topics/politics/survey-results/daily/2020/07/13/c2c8a/2.

15. Meyer, *The Politics of Protest*, 2.

16. Meyer, *The Politics of Protest*, 222.

17. Meyer, *The Politics of Protest*, 222.

18. Verba, Schlozman, and Brady, *Voice and Equality*.

19. Verba, Schlozman, and Brady, *Voice and Equality.* McVeigh and Smith, "Who Protests in America," reach similar conclusions in their analysis, finding that those who engage in protests are similar to those who engage actively in institutionalized politics (such as voting), but that education on social and political issues, participation in community organizations, and frequent church attendance increase the likelihood that individuals will engage in protest relative to institutionalized politics.

20. Meyer, *The Politics of Protest*, 222.

21. Gilens, "Public Opinion and Democratic Responsiveness."

22. Gilens and Page, "Testing Theories of American Politics."

23. Browning, Marshall, and Tabb, "Protest Is Not Enough," 240.

24. Browning, Marshall, and Tabb, "Protest Is Not Enough," 241.

25. Ballard, "Black Americans Believe Activism Is Uniting the Country"; Frankovic, "What Impact Will Racial Protests Have on America Long-Term?"

26. Intravia, Piquero, and Piquero, "The Racial Divide Surrounding United States of America National Anthem Protests in the National Football League."

27. Perry and Romer, "Protesting Is as Important as Voting."

28. Meyer, *The Politics of Protest*, 23.

29. Center for American Women and Politics (CAWP), Women Elected Officials Database, Eagleton Institute of Politics, Rutgers University, https://cawpdata.rutgers.edu/.

30. CAWP, https://cawp.rutgers.edu/shaping-history-cawp-through -years?filter=all.

31. CAWP, https://www.census.gov/quickfacts/fact/table/US/LFE 046220.

32. CAWP, https://www.census.gov/quickfacts/fact/table/US/PST 045221.

33. All of these data come from Jennifer E. Manning, *Membership of the 117th Congress: A Profile*, Congressional Research Service, updated May 25, 2022.

34. DiMock, "Defining Generations"; Fry, "Millennials Overtake Baby Boomers."

35. Center for Youth Political Participation, Young Elected Leaders Project, https://eagleton.rutgers.edu/wp-content/uploads/2019/07/YELPFullReport.pdf.

36. U.S. Census Bureau: https://www.census.gov/newsroom/press-releases/2020/2020-demographic-analysis-estimates.html.

37. Manning, *Membership of the 117th Congress.*

38. Traister, "Dianne Feinstein Fought for Gun Control"; Kilpatrick, "A Worrying Phone Call."

39. Rehfeld, "Representation Rethought," 218.

40. Mansbridge, "Rethinking Representation," 515.

41. Hayes and Hibbing, "The Symbolic Benefits of Descriptive and Substantive Representation."

42. Minta and Sinclair-Chapman, "Diversity in Political Institutions and Congressional Responsiveness to Minority Interests."

43. Lowande, Ritch, and Lauderbach, "Descriptive and Substantive Representation in Congress."

44. See Crenshaw, "Demarginalizing the Intersection of Race and Sex"; Crenshaw, "Mapping the Margins"; King, "Multiple Jeopardy, Multiple Consciousness"; McCall, "The Complexity of Intersectionality"; Junn and Brown, "What Revolution? Incorporating Intersectionality in Women and Politics."

45. An expression credited to Children's Defense Fund founder Marian Wright Edelman.

46. "Congress and the Public," Gallup, https://news.gallup.com/poll/1600/congress-public.aspx.

47. Jones, "Confidence in US Institutions Down."

48. Brenan, "Americans' Trust in Government Remains Low."

49. Open Secrets, https://www.opensecrets.org/elections-overview/election-trends.

50. Open Secrets, https://www.opensecrets.org/elections-overview/incumbent-advantage.

51. Jacobson, *The Politics of Congressional Elections,* 47.

52. Burton, Miller, and Shea, *Campaign Craft,* xxv.

53. Dittmar, Sanbonmatsu, and Carroll, *A Seat at the Table*, 60.

54. See Dittmar, Sanbonmatsu, and Carroll, *A Seat at the Table*, 60–65.

55. Ready to Run®, https://cawp.rutgers.edu/programs/ready-to-run.

56. New American Leaders, https://newamericanleaders.org/programs/ready-to-lead/.

57. Center for Youth Political Participation, https://cypp.rutgers.edu/young-leaders/.

58. Theodore Roosevelt, https://www.whitehouse.gov/about-the-white-house/presidents/theodore-roosevelt/.

59. "Citizenship in a Republic," delivered at the Sorbonne in Paris, April 23, 1910.

60. Levine, *The Future of Democracy*, 21–22.

61. Aristotle, *Politics*, chapter 1.

62. Tocqueville, *Democracy in America*, volume I, part 2, chapter 4.

63. See Verba, Schlozman, and Brady, *Voice and Equality*, 40–96.

64. Levine, *The Future of Democracy*, 17–22.

65. Verba, Schlozman, and Brady, *Voice and Equality*, 74–79.

66. Schlachter, "Key Findings from the 2019 Current Population Survey."

67. Schlachter, "Key Findings from the 2019 Current Population Survey," 4.

68. Center for Information and Research on Civic Learning and Engagement, February 3, 2022, https://circle.tufts.edu/latest-research/young-women-color-continue-lead-civic-and-political-engagement.

69. McCartney, Bennion, and Simpson, eds., *Teaching Civic Engagement*, 15.

70. Teach for America, https://www.teachforamerica.org/.

71. Rutgers Summer Service Internship initiative, https://careers.rutgers.edu/rssi.

72. AmeriCorps, https://americorps.gov/; Everyday Democracy, https://www.everyday-democracy.org/; Citizen University, https://citizenuniversity.us/.

73. Citizen University, https://citizenuniversity.us/about/story/.

74. For background on Thoreau, see https://www.loc.gov/item /today-in-history/july-12/; for background on Parks, see https://naacp .org/find-resources/history-explained/civil-rights-leaders/rosa -parks. Relevant scholarship on the contours and efficacy of civil disobedience include Brownlee, *Conscience and Conviction*; Cohen, "Civil Disobedience and the Law"; Cohen, "Civil Disobedience in Constitutional Democracy"; Rawls, *A Theory of Justice*.

75. For more on social entrepreneurship, see the Center for the Advancement of Social Entrepreneurship (CASE), https://centers .fuqua.duke.edu/case/about/what-is-social-entrepreneurship/.

CHAPTER 6 — IT DEPENDS ON US

1. Whitman, *Democratic Vistas*, xv.

2. Whitman, *Democratic Vistas*, xvi.

3. Najarro, "Revamped Florida Civics Education Aims for 'Patriotism.'"

4. See Ed Folsom and Kenneth M. Price, "Family Origins," Walt Whitman Archives, https://whitmanarchive.org/biography/walt _whitman/index.html#origins.

5. See the Walt Whitman Birthplace Association, https://www .waltwhitman.org/about/about-whitman/.

6. See Folsom and Price, "Self-Education and Early Career," Walt Whitman Archives, https://whitmanarchive.org/biography/walt _whitman/index.html#education.

7. See Folsom and Price, "Self-Education and Early Career," Walt Whitman Archives, https://whitmanarchive.org/biography/walt _whitman/index.html#education.

8. See Hutchinson and Drews, "Racial Attitudes."

9. Lott, "O'Connor, William Douglas." Referenced in Miller, "Seeing Whitman through the Eyes of Langston Hughes."

10. See Langston Hughes, https://poets.org/poet/langston-hughes.

11. Langston Hughes, "The Negro Artist and the Racial Mountain," cited in Poetry Foundation: https://www.poetryfoundation .org/articles/69395/the-negro-artist-and-the-racial-mountain.

12. Miller, "Seeing Whitman through the Eyes of Langston Hughes."

13. *Evening Courier*, Camden, New Jersey, March 3, 1927, referenced in Miller, "Seeing Whitman through the Eyes of Langston Hughes."

14. "Langston Hughes: Calls Whitman Negroes' First Great Poetic Friend, Lincoln of Letter," *Chicago Defender*, July 4, 1953, referenced in Miller, "Seeing Whitman through the Eyes of Langston Hughes."

15. "An English Professor Disagrees on Whitman's Racial Attitudes," *Chicago Defender*, July 25, 1953, referenced in Miller, "Seeing Whitman through the Eyes of Langston Hughes."

16. "Like Whitman, Great Artists Are Not Always Good People," *Chicago Defender*, August 1, 1953, referenced in Miller, "Seeing Whitman through the Eyes of Langston Hughes."

17. University of Texas at Austin, Lyndon B. Johnson School of Public Affairs, https://lbj.utexas.edu/news/2012/lbj-professor-barbara-jordans-landmark-speech-1976-democrati.

FURTHER READING

1. Smith, *How the Word Is Passed*, 289.

2. Walt Whitman Archive, https://whitmanarchive.org/.

3. Walt Whitman House, https://nj.gov/dep/parksandforests/historic/waltwhitmanhouse.html.

Bibliography

Allen, Danielle. "Liberty, Equality Aren't Mutually Exclusive." *Washington Post*, October 17, 2014. https://www.washingtonpost.com/opinions/liberty-equality-arent-mutually-exclusive/2014/10/17/d9df36ba-55fb-11e4-809b-8cc0a295c773_story.html.

———. *Our Declaration: A Reading of the Declaration of Independence in Defense of Equality.* New York: W. W. Norton, 2014.

Allen, Danielle, and Paul Carrese. "Opinion: Our Democracy Is Ailing. Civics Has to Be Part of the Cure." *Washington Post*, March 2, 2021. https://www.washingtonpost.com/opinions/2021/03/02/our-democracy-is-ailing-civics-education-has-be-part-cure/.

Alvarez, R. Michael, Stephen Ansolabehere, and Catherine H. Wilson. "Election Day Voter Registration in the United States: How One-Step Voting Can Change the Composition of the American Electorate." VTP Working Paper. Caltech/MIT Voting Technology Project, Pasadena, CA, 2002.

Ambar, Saladin. *Reconsidering American Political Thought: A New Identity.* New York: Routledge, Taylor and Francis Group, 2020.

"America Needs History and Civics Education to Promote Unity." *Wall Street Journal*, March 1, 2021. https://www.wsj.com/articles/america-needs-history-and-civics-education-to-promote-unity-11614641530.

Anishanslin, Zara. "What We Get Wrong about Ben Franklin's 'A Republic, if You Can Keep It.'" *Washington Post*, October 29, 2019. https://www.washingtonpost.com/outlook/2019/10/29/what -we-get-wrong-about-ben-franklins-republic-if-you-can-keep-it/.

Ansolabehere, Stephen, and David M. Konisky. "The Introduction of Voter Registration and Its Effect on Turnout." *Political Analysis* 14, no. 1 (2006): 83–100. http://www.jstor.org/stable/25791836.

Applebaum, Anne. *Twilight of Democracy: The Seductive Lure of Authoritarianism*. New York: Doubleday, 2021.

Aristotle. *The Complete Works of Aristotle: Politics*. Edited by Jonathan Barnes. Princeton, NJ: Princeton University Press, 1984.

Ballard, Jamie. "Black Americans Believe Activism Is Uniting the Country, but White Americans Don't Agree." *YouGov*, November 11, 2020. https://today.yougov.com/topics/politics/articles -reports/2020/11/11/activism-uniting-dividing-country-black -americans.

Bartels, Larry M. "Economic Inequality and Political Representation." In *The Unsustainable American State*, edited by Lawrence Jacobs and Desmond King. Oxford: Oxford University Press, 2009. doi: 10.1093/acprof:oso/9780195392135.003.0007.

———. "Ethnic Antagonism Erodes Republicans' Commitment to Democracy." *Proceedings of the National Academy of Sciences* 117, no. 37 (2020): 22752–22759.

Bates, Karen Grigsby. "When Civility Is Used as a Cudgel against People of Color." *Code Switch*, March 25, 2019. https://www.npr.org /sections/codeswitch/2019/03/14/700897826/when-civility-is-used -as-a-cudgel-against-people-of-color.

Baumgartner, Frank R., and Beth L. Leech. *Basic Interests: The Importance of Groups in Politics and Political Science*. Princeton, NJ: Princeton University Press, 1998.

Bennett, Kate. "Ivanka Trump Calls Rioters 'Patriots,' Then Deletes Tweet." *CNN Politics*, January 6, 2021. https://edition.cnn.com /politics/live-news/congress-electoral-college-vote-count-2021/h _c5331ac03e1575a2b8121ae9df6d56bb.

Bishop, Bill. *The Big Sort: Why the Clustering of Like-Minded America Is Tearing Us Apart*. New York: Houghton Mifflin, 2008.

Boatright, Robert G. "Introduction." In *A Crisis of Civility? Political Discourse and Its Discontents*, edited by Robert G. Boatright, Timothy J. Shaffer, Sarah Sobieraj, and Dannagal Goldthwaite Young. New York. Routledge and Taylor & Francis, 2019.

Borter, Gabriella, Joseph Ax, and Joseph Tanfani. "School Boards Get Death Threats amid Rage over Race, Gender, Mask Policies." *Reuters*, February 15, 2022. https://www.reuters.com/investigates /special-report/usa-education-threats/.

Brenan, Megan. "Americans' Trust in Government Remains Low." *Gallup*, September 30, 2021. https://news.gallup.com/poll/355124 /americans-trust-government-remains-low.aspx.

Brians, Craig Leonard, and Brian Grofman. "Election Day Registration's Effect on U.S. Voter Turnout." *Social Science Quarterly* 82 (2001): 170–183. https://doi.org/10.1111/0038-4941.00015.

Brockell, Gillian. "'A Republic, if You Can Keep It': Did Ben Franklin Really Say Impeachment Day's Favorite Quote?" *Washington Post*, December 18, 2019. https://www.washingtonpost.com/history /2019/12/18/republic-if-you-can-keep-it-did-ben-franklin-really -say-impeachment-days-favorite-quote/.

Brooks, Arthur C. "Empathize with Your Political Foe." *New York Times*, January 21, 2018. https://www.nytimes.com/2018/01/21 /opinion/empathize-with-your-political-foe.html.

Browning, Rufus P., Dale Rogers Marshall, and David H. Tabb. "Protest Is Not Enough: A Theory of Political Incorporation." *PS* 19, no. 3 (1986): 576–581. https://doi.org/10.2307/419179.

Brownlee, Kimberley. *Conscience and Conviction: The Case for Civil Disobedience*. Oxford: Oxford University Press, 2012.

Burden, Barry C., David T. Canon, Kenneth R. Mayer, and Donald P. Moynihan. "The Effects and Costs of Early Voting, Election Day Registration, and Same Day Registration in the 2008 Elections." University of Wisconsin–Madison, 2009. https://www.pewtrusts .org/~/media/legacy/uploadedfiles/pcs_assets/2009/uwisconsin1 pdf.pdf.

Burden, Barry C., and Trey Grayson. *Report on the Cyber Ninjas Review of the 2020 Presidential and U.S. Senatorial Elections in Maricopa County, Arizona.* States United Democracy Center, June 22, 2021. https://statesuniteddemocracy.org/wp-content/uploads/2021/06/6.22.21-SUDC-Report-re-Cyber-Ninjas-Review-FINAL.pdf.

Burton, Michael John, William J. Miller, and Daniel M. Shea. *Campaign Craft: The Strategies, Tactics, and Art of Political Campaign Management,* 5th ed. Westport, CT: Praeger, 2015.

Campbell, David. "Voice in the Classroom: How an Open Classroom Environment Facilitates Adolescents' Civic Development." Working Paper 28. Center for Information and Research on Civic Learning and Engagement, 2005. https://civicyouth.org/circle-working-paper-28-voice-in-the-classroom-how-an-open-classroom-environment-facilitates-adolescents-civic-development/.

Carnegie Corporation of New York. "Voting Rights: A Short History." Carnegie Corporation, November 18, 2019. https://www.carnegie.org/our-work/article/voting-rights-timeline/.

Censk, Abigail. "Heavily Armed Protesters Gather Again at Michigan Capitol to Decry Stay-at-Home Order." *NPR,* May 14, 2020. https://www.npr.org/2020/05/14/855918852/heavily-armed-protesters-gather-again-at-michigans-capitol-denouncing-home-order.

Center for Information and Research on Civic Learning and Engagement (CIRCLE). "Election Week 2020: Young People Increase Turnout, Lead Biden to Victory." November 25, 2020. https://circle.tufts.edu/latest-research/election-week-2020#youth-voter-turnout-increased-in-2020.

———. "Half of Youth Voted in 2020, an 11-Point Increase from 2016." April 29, 2021. https://circle.tufts.edu/latest-research/half-youth-voted-2020-11-point-increase-2016.

———. "State-by-State 2020 Youth Voter Turnout: The Northeast." April 13, 2021. https://circle.tufts.edu/latest-research/state-state-2020-youth-voter-turnout-northeast.

Chemerinsky, Erwin, and Howard Gillman. *Free Speech on Campus.* New Haven, CT: Yale University Press, 2017.

Chiacu, Doina. "Republicans Censure Cheney, Kinzinger, Call Jan. 6 Probe Attack on 'Legitimate Political Discourse.'" *Reuters*, February 4, 2022. https://www.reuters.com/world/us/loyal-trump -republican-party-moves-censure-us-reps-cheney-kinzinger -2022-02-04/.

Chokshi, Niraj. "What College Students Really Think about Free Speech." *New York Times*, March 12, 2018. https://www.nytimes .com/2018/03/12/us/college-students-free-speech.html.

Cineas, Fabiola. "The Insurrection Is Happening at State Capitols, Too." *Vox*, January 6, 2021. https://www.vox.com/2021/1/6/22217736 /state-capitol-stop-the-steal-protests-rallies.

Cohen, Andrew. "Representative John Lewis: 'Make Some Noise' on New Voting Restrictions." *The Atlantic*, August 26, 2012. https:// www.theatlantic.com/politics/archive/2012/08/rep-john-lewis -make-some-noise-on-new-voting-restrictions/261549/.

Cohen, Carl. "Civil Disobedience and the Law." *Rutgers Law Review* 21, no. 1 (1966): 1–17.

Cohen, Marshall. "Civil Disobedience in Constitutional Democracy." *Philosophic Exchange* 1 no. 1 (1970): 99–110.

Colby, Anne, Thomas Ehrlich, Elizabeth Beaumont, and Jason Stephens. *Educating Citizens: Preparing America's Undergraduates for Lives of Moral and Civic Responsibility.* San Francisco: Jossey-Bass, 2003.

Crenshaw, Kimberle. "Demarginalizing the Intersection of Race and Sex: A Black Feminist Critique of Antidiscrimination Doctrine, Feminist Theory and Antiracist Politics." *University of Chicago Legal Forum* 1989 (1989): 139–167.

———. "Mapping the Margins: Intersectionality, Identity Politics, and Violence against Women of Color." *Stanford Law Review* 43, no. 6 (1991): 1241–1299. https://doi.org/10.2307/1229039.

Dent, Charlie, Mary Peters, Denver Riggleman, Michael Steele, and Christine Todd Whitman. "Opinion: The GOP Has Lost Its Way. Fellow Americans, Join Our New Alliance." *Washington Post*, May 13, 2021. https://www.washingtonpost.com/opinions/2021/05 /13/new-gop-alliance-dent-peters-riggleman-steele-whitman.

DeSilver, Drew. "In Past Elections, U.S. Trailed Most Developed Countries in Voter Turnout." Pew Research Center, November 3, 2022. https://www.pewresearch.org/fact-tank/2020/11/03/in-past-elections-u-s-trailed-most-developed-countries-in-voter-turnout/.

———. "Turnout Soared in 2020 as Nearly Two-Thirds of Eligible U.S. Voters Cast Ballots for President." Pew Research Center, January 28, 2021. https://www.pewresearch.org/fact-tank/2021/01/28/turnout-soared-in-2020-as-nearly-two-thirds-of-eligible-u-s-voters-cast-ballots-for-president/.

DiMock, Michael. "Defining Generations: Where Millennials End and Generation Z Begins." Pew Research Center, January 17, 2019. https://www.pewresearch.org/fact-tank/2019/01/17/where-millennials-end-and-generation-z-begins/.

Dittmar, Kelly, Kira Sanbonmatsu, and Susan J. Carroll. *A Seat at the Table: Congresswomen's Perspectives on Why Their Presence Matters*. New York: Oxford University Press, 2018.

Editorial Board. "America Must Embrace Civics and History Instruction for the Sake of Our Democracy." *Washington Post*, March 2, 2021. https://www.washingtonpost.com/opinions/america-must-embrace-civics-and-history-instruction-for-the-sake-of-our-democracy/2021/03/02/b9814476-7877-11eb-9537-496158cc5fd9_story.html.

Feierherd, German, Noam Lupu, and Susan Stokes. "A Significant Minority of Americans Say They Could Support a Military Takeover of the U.S. Government." *Washington Post, Monkey Cage Blog*, February 16, 2018. https://www.washingtonpost.com/news/monkey-cage/wp/2018/02/16/a-significant-minority-of-americans-say-they-would-support-a-military-takeover-of-the-u-s-in-the-right-circumstances/.

Fenster, Mark J. "The Impact of Allowing Day of Registration Voting on Turnout in U.S. Elections from 1960 to 1992: A Research Note." *American Politics Quarterly* 22, no. 1 (1994): 74–87. https://doi.org/10.1177/1532673X9402200105.

Frankovic, Kathy. "What Impact Will Racial Protests Have on America Long-Term?" *YouGov*, July 10, 2020. https://today.yougov.com

/topics/politics/articles-reports/2020/07/10/impact-protests
-america.

Freedom House. *Freedom in the World 2021: Democracy under
Siege*. 2021. https://freedomhouse.org/sites/default/files/2021-02
/FIW2021_World_02252021_FINAL-web-upload.pdf.

Friedman, Milton. *Free to Choose: A Personal Statement*. New York:
Harcourt, 1980.

Frum, David. "The Founders Were Wrong about Democracy." *The
Atlantic*, February 15, 2021. https://www.theatlantic.com/ideas
/archive/2021/02/america-must-become-democracy/618028/.

Fry, Richard. "Millennials Overtake Baby Boomers as America's
Largest Generation." Pew Research Center, April 28, 2020. https://
www.pewresearch.org/fact-tank/2020/04/28/millennials
-overtake-baby-boomers-as-americas-largest-generation/.

Gilens, Martin. "Public Opinion and Democratic Responsiveness:
Who Gets What They Want." Russell Sage Foundation, n.d. https://
www.russellsage.org/sites/all/files/u4/Gilens.pdf.

Gilens, Martin, and Benjamin I. Page. "Testing Theories of American
Politics: Elites, Interest Groups, and Average Citizens." *Perspectives
on Politics* 12, no. 3 (2014): 564–581. doi: 10.1017/S1537592714001595.

Gilliam, Franklin D., Jr. "Influences on Voter Turnout for U. S. House
Elections in Non-Presidential Years." *Legislative Studies Quarterly*
10 (1985): 339–351.

Gómez, Vianney, and Carroll Doherty. "Wide Partisan Divide on
Whether Voting Is a Fundamental Right or a Privilege with
Responsibilities." Pew Research Center, July 22, 2021. https://www
.pewresearch.org/fact-tank/2021/07/22/wide-partisan-divide-on
-whether-voting-is-a-fundamental-right-or-a-privilege-with
-responsibilities/.

Gould, Jonathan, Kathleen Hall Jamieson, Peter Levine, Ted McCo-
nnell, and David B. Smith, eds. *Guardian of Democracy: The Civic
Mission of Schools*. Philadelphia: Leonore Annenberg Institute for
Civics, 2011.

Grey, Kathleen. "In Michigan, a Dress Rehearsal for the Chaos at the
Capitol on Wednesday." *New York Times*, January 9, 2021. https://

www.nytimes.com/2021/01/09/us/politics/michigan-state-capitol
.html.

Gronke, Paul, Eva Galanes-Rosenbaum, and Peter A. Miller. "Early Voting and Turnout." *PS* 40 (2007): 639–645.

Haberman, Maggie, and Michael D. Shear. "Trump Signs Executive Order Protecting Free Speech on College Campuses." *New York Times*, March 21, 2019. https://www.nytimes.com/2019/03/21/us /politics/trump-free-speech-executive-order.html.

Hamilton, Alexander, James Madison, and John Jay. *The Federalist Papers*. Edited by Clinton Rossiter. New York: Mentor Books, 1961.

Hand, Learned. "I Am an American Day." In *Become America: Civic Sermons on Love, Responsibility, and Democracy*, by Eric Liu. Seattle: Sasquatch Books, 2019.

Hanmer, Michael J. *Discount Voting: Voter Registration Reforms and Their Effects*. New York: Cambridge University Press, 2009.

Hardy, Henry, ed. *The Crooked Timber of Humanity: Chapters in the History of Ideas*. Princeton, NJ: Princeton University Press, 2013.
———, ed. *Liberty*. Oxford: Oxford University Press, 2002.

Hayes, Matthew, and Matthew V. Hibbing. "The Symbolic Benefits of Descriptive and Substantive Representation." *Political Behavior* 39 (2016): 31–50. https://doi.org/10.1007/s11109-016-9345-9.

Heim, Joe. "Massive Investment in Social Studies and Civics Education Proposed to Address Eroding Trust in Democratic Institutions." *Washington Post*, March 1, 2021. https://www.washingtonpost .com/education/civics-social-studies-education-plan/2021/03/01 /e245e34a-747f-11eb-9537-496158cc5fd9_story.html.

Helzer, Erik. "Try Fact-Checking Yourself for a Change." *Baltimore Sun*, February 3, 2017. https://www.baltimoresun.com/opinion/op -ed/bs-ed-factchecking-yourself-20170204-story.html.

Hess, Diana E. *Controversy in the Classroom: The Democratic Power of Discussion*. New York: Routledge, 2009.

Hess, Diana E., and Paula McAvoy. *The Political Classroom: Evidence and Ethics in Democratic Education*. New York: Routledge, 2014.

Highton, Benjamin. "Revisiting the Relationship between Educational Attainment and Political Sophistication." *Journal of Politics*

71, no. 4 (2009): 1564–1576. https://doi.org/10.1017/S002238160
9990077.

Hutchinson, George, and David Drews. "Racial Attitudes." In *Walt Whitman: An Encyclopedia*, edited by J. R. LeMaster and Donald D. Kummings. New York: Garland Publishing, 1998. https://whitmanarchive.org/criticism/current/encyclopedia/entry_44.html.

Intravia, Jonathan, Alex R. Piquero, and Nicole Leeper Piquero. "The Racial Divide Surrounding United States of America National Anthem Protests in the National Football League." *Deviant Behavior* 39, no. 8 (2018): 1058–1068. https://doi.org/10.1080/01639625.2017.1399745.

Jacobson, Gary C. *The Politics of Congressional Elections*, 8th ed. Upper Saddle River, NJ: Pearson, 2012.

Jones, Jeffrey M. "Confidence in US Institutions Down; Average at New Low." *Gallup*, July 5, 2022. https://news.gallup.com/poll/394283/confidence-institutions-down-average-new-low.aspx.

Junn, Jane, and Nadia Brown. 2008. "What Revolution? Incorporating Intersectionality in Women and Politics." In *Political Women and American Democracy*, edited by Christina Wolbrecht, Karen Beckwith, and Lisa Baldez, 64–78. New York: Cambridge University Press.

Kahne, Joseph, and Ellen Middaugh. "Democracy for Some: The Civic Opportunity Gap in High School." Center for Information and Research on Civic Learning and Engagement (CIRCLE), February 26, 2008. https://circle.tufts.edu/sites/default/files/2019-12/WP59_TheCivicOpportunityGapinHighSchool_2008.pdf.

Kelley, Stanley, Jr., Richard E. Ayres, and William G. Bowen. "Registration and Voting: Putting First Things First." *American Political Science Review* 61 (1967): 359–379.

Kenski, Kate, Kevin Cole, and Stephen A. Rains. "Perceptions of Incivility in Public Discourse." In *A Crisis of Civility? Political Discourse and Its Discontents*, edited by Robert G. Boatright, Timothy J. Shaffer, Sarah Sobieraj, and Dannagal Goldthwaite Young. New York: Routledge and Taylor & Francis, 2019.

Khavin, Dmitry, Haley Willis, Evan Hill, Natatlie Reneau, Drew Jordan, Cora Engelbrecht, Christiaan Triebert, Stella Cooper, Malachy Browne, and David Botti. "A Day of Rage: An In-Depth Look at How a Mob Stormed the Capitol." *New York Times*, June 30, 2021. https://www.nytimes.com/video/us/politics/100000007606996/capitol-riot-trump-supporters.html?smtyp=cur&smid=tw-nytimes.

Kilpatrick, Amina. "A Worrying Phone Call Adds to Concerns about Sen. Dianne Feinstein's Cognitive Health." *NPR*, June 13, 2022. https://www.npr.org/2022/06/13/1104843151/senator-dianne-feinstein-cognitive-health-continues-to-raise-concerns-traister.

King, Deborah K. "Multiple Jeopardy, Multiple Consciousness: The Context of a Black Feminist Ideology." *Signs: Journal of Women in Culture and Society* 14, no. 1 (1988): 42–72. https://doi.org/10.1086/494491.

Knack, Stephen. "Election-Day Registration: The Second Wave." *American Politics Research* 29 (2001): 65–78.

Knight Foundation. "Free Expression on Campus: What College Students Think about First Amendment Issues." March 12, 2018. https://knightfoundation.org/reports/free-expression-on-campus-what-college-students-think-about-first-amendment-issues.

Laden, Anthony Simon. "Two Concepts of Civility." In *A Crisis of Civility? Political Discourse and Its Discontents*, edited by Robert G. Boatright, Timothy J. Shaffer, Sarah Sobieraj, and Dannagal Goldthwaite Young. New York. Routledge and Taylor & Francis, 2019.

Levendusky, Matthew, and Dominik A. Stecula. *We Need to Talk: How Cross-Party Dialogue Reduces Affective Polarization*. Cambridge: Cambridge University Press, 2021.

Levine, Peter. *The Future of Democracy: Developing the Next Generation of American Citizens*. Medford, MA: Tufts University Press, 2007.

Levinson, Sanford. *Our Undemocratic Constitution: Where the Constitution Goes Wrong (and How We the People Can Correct It)*. Oxford: Oxford University Press, 2008.

Levitsky, Steven, and Daniel Ziblatt. *How Democracies Die*. New York: Crown Books, 2019.

Lott, Deshae E. "O'Connor, William Douglas [1832–1889]." In *Walt Whitman: An Encyclopedia*, edited by J. R. LeMaster and Donald D. Kummings. New York: Garland Publishing, 1998.

Lowande, Kenneth, Melinda Ritchie, and Erinn Lauterbach. "Descriptive and Substantive Representation in Congress: Evidence from 80,000 Congressional Inquiries." *American Journal of Political Science* 63, no. 3 (2019): 644–659. http://www.jstor.org /stable/45132502.

Macedo, Stephen, ed. *Democracy at Risk: How Political Choices Undermine Citizen Participation and What We Can Do about It*. Washington, DC: Brookings Institution Press, 2005.

Mann, Thomas E., and Norm J. Ornstein. *It's Even Worse Than It Looks: How the American Constitutional System Collided with the New Politics of Extremism*. New York: Basic Books, 2016.

Mansbridge, Jane. "Rethinking Representation." *American Political Science Review* 97, no. 4 (2003): 515–528.

Matto, Elizabeth C. *Citizen Now: Engaging in Politics and Democracy*. Manchester, UK: Manchester University Press, 2017.

———. "Civics Education Is the Best Way to Prevent the Next Attack on American Democracy." *NJ.com*, January 28, 2021. https://www.nj.com/opinion/2021/01/civics-education-is-the-best -way-to-prevent-the-next-attack-on-american-democracy -opinion.html.

Matto, Elizabeth C., and Randi Chmielewski. "Talking Politics: Creating a Course for Incoming Freshman on Political Discourse." *Journal of Political Science Education* 17 (2021): 751–761. https://doi .org/10.1080/15512169.2020.1818575.

Matto, Elizabeth C., Alison Rios Millett McCartney, Elizabeth A. Bennion, Alasdair Blair, Taiyi Sun, and Dawn Whitehead, eds. *Teaching Civic Engagement Globally*. Washington, DC: American Political Science Association, 2021.

Matto, Elizabeth C., Alison Rios Millett McCartney, Elizabeth A. Bennion, and Dick Simpson, eds. *Teaching Civic Engagement across the Disciplines.* Washington, DC: American Political Science Association, 2017.

Mayhew, David R. *Congress: The Electoral Connection*, 2nd ed. New Haven, CT: Yale University Press, 2005.

McCall, Leslie. "The Complexity of Intersectionality." *Signs: Journal of Women in Culture and Society* 30, no. 3 (2005): 1771–1800. https://doi.org/10.1086/426800.

McCartney, Alison Rios Millett, Elizabeth A. Bennion, and Dick Simpson, eds. *Teaching Civic Engagement: From Student to Active Citizen.* Washington, DC: American Political Science Association, 2013.

McDevitt, Michael, and Spiro Kiousis. "Experiments in Political Socialization: Kids Voting USA as a Model for Civic Education Reform." Working Paper 49. Center for Information and Research on Civic Learning and Engagement, 2006. https://civicyouth.org/circle-working-paper-49-experiments-in-political-socialization-kids-voting-usa-as-a-model-for-civic-education-reform/.

McVeigh, Rory, and Christian Smith. "Who Protests in America: An Analysis of Three Political Alternatives—Inaction, Institutionalized Politics, or Protest." *Sociological Forum* 14, no. 4 (1999): 685–702. http://www.jstor.org/stable/685079.

Meyer, David S. *The Politics of Protest: Social Movements in America*, 2nd ed. New York: Oxford University Press, 2015.

Mikell, Ray. "Methods Discussion and Active Learning in a Volatile Age: A Reflection and Analysis." *Journal of Political Science Education* 15, no. 2 (2019): 247–256. https://doi.org/10.1080/15512169.2018.1464928.

Miller, Pauline. "Seeing Whitman through the Eyes of Langston Hughes." *Conversations: Newsletter of the Walt Whitman Association*, Spring 2021, 1–7.

Minta, Michael D., and Valeria Sinclair-Chapman. "Diversity in Political Institutions and Congressional Responsiveness to Minority Interests." *Political Research Quarterly* 66, no. 1 (March 2013): 127–140. https://www.jstor.org/stable/23563594.

Mitchell, Glenn E., and Christopher Wlezien. "The Impact of Legal Constraints on Voter Registration, Turnout, and the Composition of the American Electorate." *Political Behavior* 17 (1995): 179–202.

Morris, Kevin, Myrna Pérez, John Brater, and Christopher Deluzio. "Purges: A Growing Threat to the Right to Vote." Brennan Center for Justice, July 20, 2018. https://www.brennancenter.org/our-work /research-reports/state-voting-2018.

Moyers, John. "John Lewis Marches On." *Moyers & Company*, August 21, 2022. https://billmoyers.com/episode/john-lewis -marches-on/.

Muddiman, Ashley. "How People Perceive Political Inactivity." In *A Crisis of Civility? Political Discourse and Its Discontents*, edited by Robert G. Boatright, Timothy J. Shaffer, Sarah Sobieraj, and Dannagal Goldthwaite Young. New York: Routledge and Taylor & Francis, 2019.

Mutz, Diana. *Hearing the Other Side: Deliberative versus Participatory Democracy*. New York: Cambridge University Press, 2006.

Najarro, Ileana. "Revamped Florida Civics Education Aims for 'Patriotism.' Will It Catch On Elsewhere?" *Education Week*, July 12, 2022. https://www.edweek.org/teaching-learning/revamped-florida -civics-education-aims-for-patriotism-will-it-catch-on-elsewhere /2022/07.

National Task Force on Civic Learning and Engagement. *A Crucible Moment: College Learning and Democracy's Future*. Washington, DC: American Association of Colleges and Universities, 2012. https://www.aacu.org/publication/a-crucible-moment-college -learning-democracys-future.

New America. "Statement of Concern: The Threats to American Democracy and the Need for National Voting and Election Administration Standards." June 1, 2021. https://www.newamerica.org /political-reform/statements/statement-of-concern/.

Nichols, Mark. "Closed Voting Sites Hit Minority Counties Harder for Busy Midterm Elections." *USA Today*, October 30, 2018. https://

www.usatoday.com/story/news/2018/10/30/midterm-elections
-closed-voting-sites-impact-minority-voter-turnout/1774221002/.

Oros, Andrew L. "Let's Debate: Active Learning Encourages Student
Participation and Critical Thinking." *Journal of Political Science
Education* 3, no. 3 (2007): 293–311.

Panke, Stefanie, and J. Stephens. "Beyond the Echo Chamber: Peda-
gogical Tools for Civic Engagement Discourse and Reflection."
Journal of Educational Technology and Society 21 (2018): 248–263.

Perry, Andre M., and Carl Romer, "Protesting Is as Important as
Voting." Brookings Institution, August 28, 2020. https://www
.brookings.edu/blog/the-avenue/2020/08/28/protesting-is-as
-important-as-voting/.

Pew Research Center. "More Now Say It's 'Stressful' to Discuss Politics with People They Disagree With." November 5, 2018. https://
www.pewresearch.org/politics/2018/11/05/more-now-say-its
-stressful-to-discuss-politics-with-people-they-disagree-with/.

———. "Partisan Antipathy: More Intense, More Personal." October 10, 2019. https://www.pewresearch.org/politics/wp-content
/uploads/sites/4/2019/10/10-10-19-Parties-report.pdf.

———. "Public Highly Critical of State of Political Discourse in the
U.S." June 19, 2019. https://www.pewresearch.org/politics/2019/06
/19/public-highly-critical-of-state-of-political-discourse-in-the-u-s/.

———. "The Public, the Political System and American Democracy:
Most Say 'Design and Structure' Need Big Changes." April 26, 2018.
https://assets.pewresearch.org/wp-content/uploads/sites/5/2018
/04/26140617/4-26-2018-Democracy-release.pdf.

———. "Republicans and Democrats Move Further Apart in Views
of Voting Access." April 22, 2021. https://www.pewresearch.org
/politics/2021/04/22/republicans-and-democrats-move-further
-apart-in-views-of-voting-access/.

———. "Sharp Divisions on Vote Counts, as Biden Gets High Marks
for His Post-Election Conduct." November 20, 2020. https://www
.pewresearch.org/politics/2020/11/20/sharp-divisions-on-vote
-counts-as-biden-gets-high-marks-for-his-post-election-conduct/.

Philips, Amber. "How to Talk about Politics This Thanksgiving." *Washington Post*, November 25, 2021. https://www.washingtonpost .com/politics/2021/11/25/how-talk-about-politics-this-thanks giving/.

Pitkin, Hanna Fenichel. *The Concept of Representation*. Berkeley: University of California Press, 1967.

Powell, G. Bingham. "American Voter Turnout in Comparative Per- spective." *American Political Science Review* 80, no. 1 (1986): 17–43. https://doi.org/10.2307/1957082.

Prothro, James W., and Charles M. Grigg. "Fundamental Principles of Democracy: Bases of Agreement and Disagreement." *Journal of Politics* 22 no. 2 (1960): 276–294.

Przeworski, Adam. *Crises of Democracy*. Cambridge: Cambridge University Press, 2019.

Rawls, John. *A Theory of Justice*, rev ed. Cambridge, MA: Harvard University Press, 1999 [1971].

Rehfeld, Andrew. "Representation Rethought: On Trustees, Dele- gates, and Gyroscopes in the Study of Political Representation and Democracy." *American Political Science Review* 103, no. 2 (2009): 214–230. http://www.jstor.org/stable/27798498.

Rhine, Staci L. "Registration Reform and Turnout Change in the American States." *American Politics Quarterly* 23 (1995): 409–426.

Riker, William H. "The Two-Party System and Duverger's Law: An Essay on the History of Political Science." *American Political Sci- ence Review* 76, no. 4 (1982): 753–766.

Rojas, Hernando. "Strategy versus Understanding: How Orientations toward Political Conversation Influence Political Engagement." *Communication Research* 35 (2008): 452–480.

Rosenstone, Steven J., and John Mark Hansen. *Mobilization, Par- ticipation, and American Democracy*. Upper Saddle River, NJ: Pearson, 1993.

Rosenstone, Steven J., and Raymond E. Wolfinger. "The Effect of Reg- istration Laws on Voter Turnout." *American Political Science Review* 72, no. 1 (1978): 22–45. doi: 10.2307/1953597.

Rubin, Beth C. *Making Citizens: Transforming Civic Learning for Diverse Social Studies Classrooms*. New York: Routledge, 2012.

———. "'There's Still Not Justice': Youth Civic Identity Development amid Distinct School and Community Contexts." *Teachers College Record* 109 no. 2 (2007): 449–481.

Russonello, Giovanni. "A Thanksgiving Myth Debunked: People Aren't Fighting about Politics." *New York Times*, November 26, 2020. https://www.nytimes.com/2020/11/26/us/politics/thanks giving-politics-family-argument.html.

Sachs, Jeffrey. "Steep Rise in Gag Orders, Many Sloppily Drafted." *PEN America*, January 24, 2022. https://pen.org/steep-rise-gag -orders-many-sloppily-drafted/.

Safer, Jeanne. "How to Keep Politics Out of Thanksgiving 2020: Pass the Turkey, Not the Touchy Subjects." *USA Today*, November 13, 2020. https://www.usatoday.com/story/opinion/2020/11/13/thanks giving-dinner-politics-family-advice-avoid-fights-column/6256 133002/.

Schlachter, Laura Hanson. "Key Findings from the 2019 Current Population Survey: Civic Engagement and Volunteering Supplement." Washington, DC: AmeriCorps, Office of Research and Evaluation, 2021.

Schonfeld, Zach. "Threats to Democracy Tops List of Issues Facing US: Poll." *The Hill*, August 22, 2022. https://thehill.com/homenews /campaign/3610753-threats-to-democracy-top-list-of-issues -facing-us-poll/.

Searing, Donald D., Frederick Solt, Pamela Johnston Conover, and Ivor Crewe. "Public Discussion in the Deliberative System: Does It Make Better Citizens?" *British Journal of Political Science* 37, no. 4 (2007): 587–618.

Shaffer, Timothy J., Nicholas V. Longo, Edith Manosevitch, and Maxine S. Thomas. *Deliberative Pedagogy: Teaching and Learning for Democratic Engagement*. East Lansing: Michigan State University Press, 2017.

Smith, Clint. *How the Word Is Passed: A Reckoning with the History of Slavery across America*. New York: Little, Brown, and Company, 2021.

Smith, Elizabeth S., and Alison Bressler. "Who Taught You to Talk Like That? The University and Online Political Discourse." *Journal of Political Science Education* 9, no. 4 (2013): 453–473.

So, Linda. "Trump-Inspired Death Threats Are Terrorizing Election Workers." *Reuters*, June 11, 2021. https://www.reuters.com/investigates/section/campaign-of-fear/.

Squire, Peverill, Raymond E. Wolfinger, and David P. Glass. "Residential Mobility and Voter Turnout." *American Political Science Review* 81, no. 1 (1987): 45–65. doi: 10.2307/1960778.

Thomas, Nancy. "Educating for Democracy in Undemocratic Contexts: Avoiding the Zero-Sum Game of Campus Free Speech versus Inclusion." *eJournal of Public Affairs* 7, no. 1 (2018): 81–107. https://ejournalofpublicaffairs.org/wp-content/uploads/2018/04/EJOPA_7.1_199-Nancy-Thomas.pdf.

Thomas, Nancy, and Mark Brimhall-Vargas. *Facilitating Political Discussions*. Institute for Democracy and Higher Education, Tufts University, 2018. https://ctb.ku.edu/sites/default/files/chapter_files/facilitating_political_dialogues_workshop.pdf.

Timpone, Richard T. "Structure, Behavior, and Voter Turnout in the United States." *American Political Science Review* 92 (1998): 145–58.

Tocqueville, Alexis de. *Democracy in America and Two Essays on America*. London: Penguin Classics, 2003.

Traister, Rebecca. "Dianne Feinstein Fought for Gun Control, Civil Rights, and Abortion Access for Half a Century. Where Did It All Go Wrong? *The Cut*, June 6, 2022. https://www.thecut.com/article/dianne-feinstein-abortion-gun-civil-rights.html.

Van Green, Ted. "Republicans and Democrats Alike Say It's Stressful to Talk Politics with People Who Disagree." Pew Research Center, November 23, 2021. https://www.pewresearch.org/fact-tank/2021/11/23/republicans-and-democrats-alike-say-its-stressful-to-talk-politics-with-people-who-disagree/.

Verba, Sidney, and Norman H. Nie. *Participation in America: Political Democracy and Social Equality*. Chicago: University of Chicago Press, 1972.

Verba, Sidney, Kay Lehman Schlozman, and Henry E. Brady. *Voice and Equality: Civic Voluntarism in American Politics.* Cambridge, MA: Harvard University Press, 1995.

Victor, Jennifer N. "Democracy Is an Individual Trait." *Mischiefs of Faction*, May 31, 2020. https://www.mischiefsoffaction.com/post /democracy-is-an-individual-trait.

Vormann, Boris. and Michael D. Weinman, eds. *The Emergence of Illiberalism: Understanding a Global Phenomenon.* London: Routledge, 2020.

Wallace, Jon, Hans Kundnani, and Elizabeth Donnelly. "The Importance of Democracy: Why Is Democracy Important to the World and How Does It Help Maintain a Just and Free Society?" Chatham House, April 14, 2021. https://www.chathamhouse.org/2021/04 /importance-democracy.

Wehle, Kim. *What You Need to Know about Voting and Why.* New York: Harper, 2020.

Weiser, Wendy R. and Max Fields. "The State of Voting 2018." Brennan Center for Justice, June 5, 2018. https://www.brennancenter.org /our-work/research-reports/state-voting-2018.

Whitman, Walt. *Democratic Vistas.* Edited by Ed Folsom. Iowa City: University of Iowa Press, 2010.

Wolfinger, Raymond E., and Steven J. Rosenstone. *Who Votes?* New Haven, CT: Yale University Press, 1980.

Zukin, Cliff, Scott Keeter, Molly Andolina, Krista Jenkins, and Michael X. Delli Carpini. *A New Engagement? Political Participation, Civic Life, and the Changing American Citizen.* Oxford: Oxford University Press, 2006.

Index

About the Author

ELIZABETH C. MATTO is a research professor and director of Rutgers University's Eagleton Institute of Politics. She was the lead editor for *Teaching Civic Engagement across the Disciplines* and *Teaching Civic Engagement Globally* and is the author of *Citizen Now: Engaging in Politics and Democracy.*

ABOUT THE AUTHOR